170 FAMILY MEALS

the best-ever step-by-step recipe collection

170 FAMILY MEALS

the best-ever step-by-step recipe collection

Delicious, home-cooked favourite dishes for every day and every occasion, with over 200 mouthwatering photographs

EDITED BY MARTHA DAY

southwater

This edition is published by Southwater, an imprint of Anness Publishing Ltd,
Hermes House, 88–89 Blackfriars Road, London SE1 8HA
tel. 020 7401 2077; fax 020 7633 9499

www.southwaterbooks.com; www.annesspublishing.com

If you like the images in this book and would like to investigate using them for
publishing, promotions or advertising, please visit our website
www.practicalpictures.com for more information.

UK agent: The Manning Partnership Ltd
tel. 01225 478444; fax 01225 478440; sales@manning-partnership.co.uk
UK distributor: Grantham Book Services Ltd
tel. 01476 541080; fax 01476 541061; orders@gbs.tbs-ltd.co.uk
North American agent/distributor: National Book Network
tel. 301 459 3366; fax 301 429 5746; www.nbnbooks.com
Australian agent/distributor: Pan Macmillan Australia
tel. 1300 135 113; fax 1300 135 103; customer.service@macmillan.com.au
New Zealand agent/distributor: David Bateman Ltd
tel. (09) 415 7664; fax (09) 415 8892

Publisher: Joanna Lorenz
Editorial Director: Helen Sudell
Editor: Elizabeth Woodland
Production Controller: Don Campaniello
Design: SMI
Cover Design: Nigel Partridge
Photographers: Karl Adamson, Edward Allwright, Steve Baxter,
James Duncan, Michelle Garrett, Amanda Heywood, Don Last,
Patrick McLeavy, Michael Michaels
Additional photography: Sopexa UK
Recipes: Carla Capalbo, Maxine Clark, Frances Cleary, Carole Clements,
Roz Denny, Christine France, Sarah Gates, Shirley Gill, Rosamund Grant,
Sue Maggs, Annie Nichols, Jenny Stacey, Liz Trigg, Hilaire Walden,
Laura Washburn, Steven Wheeler, Elizabeth Wolf-Cohen
Food for Photography: Joanne Craig, Wendy Lee, Jenny Shapter, Jane Stevenson,
Elizabeth Wolf-Cohen
Home Economists: Carla Capalbo, Jenny Shapter
Stylists: Madeleine Brehaut, Carla Capalbo, Michelle Garrett, Hilary Guy, Amanda
Heywood, Blake Minton, Kirsty Rawlings, Rebecca Sturrock, Fiona Tillett

© Anness Publishing Ltd 2008

Ethical Trading Policy

At Anness Publishing we believe that business should be conducted in an ethical
and ecologically sustainable way, with respect for the environment and a proper
regard to the replacement of the natural resources we employ.

As a publisher, we use a lot of wood pulp to make high-quality paper for
printing, and that wood commonly comes from spruce trees. We are therefore
currently growing more than 500,000 trees in two Scottish forest plantations
near Aberdeen – Berrymoss (130 hectares/320 acres) and West Touxhill (125
hectares/305 acres). The forests we manage contain twice the number of trees
employed each year in paper-making for our books.

Because of this ongoing ecological investment programme, you, as our
customer, can have the pleasure and reassurance of knowing that a tree is being
cultivated on your behalf to naturally replace the materials used to make the
book you are holding.

Our forestry programme is run in accordance with the UK Woodland
Assurance Scheme (UKWAS) and will be certified by the internationally
recognized Forest Stewardship Council (FSC). The FSC is a non-government
organization dedicated to promoting responsible management of the world's
forests. Certification ensures forests are managed in an environmentally
sustainable and socially responsible basis. For further information about this
scheme, go to www.annesspublishing.com/trees

Notes

Bracketed terms are intended for American readers.
For all recipes, quantities are given in both metric and imperial measures and,
where appropriate, in standard cups and spoons. Follow one set, but not a
mixture, because they are not interchangeable.
Standard spoon and cup measures are level.
1 tsp = 5ml, 1 tbsp = 15ml, 1 cup = 250ml/8fl oz.
Australian standard tablespoons are 20ml. Australian readers should use 3 tsp in
place of 1 tbsp for measuring small quantities of gelatine, flour, salt etc.
American pints are 16fl oz/2 cups. American readers should use 20fl oz/2½ cups
in place of 1 pint when measuring liquids.
Electric oven temperatures in this book are for conventional ovens. When using
a fan oven, the temperature will probably need to be reduced by about
10–20°C/20–40°F. Since ovens vary, you should check with your manufacturer's
instruction book for guidance.
The nutritional analysis given for each recipe is calculated per portion
(i.e. serving or item), unless otherwise stated. If the recipe gives a range,
such as Serves 4–6, then the nutritional analysis will be for the smaller
portion size, i.e. serves 6.
Medium (US large) eggs are used unless otherwise stated.

Previously published as part of a larger volume, *500 Best-Ever Recipes*

Front cover shows Beef Stew with Red Wine – for recipe see page 65.

Contents

Introduction

Delicous food and the company of family and friends are two important elements of any home-cooked meal, and this cookbook provides a wealth of wonderful dishes that everyone will enjoy.

Here you will find lots of tempting dishes that are easy to make that can either be cooked within minutes, or can be prepared ahead of time ready to pop in the oven when needed. The recipes will appeal to all members of the family, whether young or not-so-young. There are plenty of interesting ideas to try, such as Nutty Cheese Balls, Chilli Prawns, and Stuffed Fish Rolls, to tempt even the most particular eater; as well as lots of filling fare to satisfy the heartiest appetites.

This volume includes a fine selection of classic dishes, each perfect for the whole family to enjoy. Many are long-standing favourites, such as Chicken and Ham Pie, Skewers of Lamb with Mint, Farmhouse Pizza, and Fish and Chips. Others are less well-known, such as Louisiana Rice, Rabbit with Mustard, Spatchcocked Devilled Poussin, and Sausage and Bean Ragoût.

Every recipe has simple, step-by-step instructions clearly explaining the techniques and cooking methods. The dishes use many accessible fresh ingredients and convenient kitchen stand-bys, ensuring that this mouthwatering collection is something no family cook should be without. Even more appealing is that many of these recipes are healthy too, and nutritional information is given for each one to help you plan and maintain a low-fat eating programme.

The book is divided into six chapters according to the type of food or course. On the savoury side, there are soups, appetizers and salads; marvellous main courses with fish and shellfish, poultry and game, and meat. There's no doubt that pasta, pizza and grains are increasingly popular and you'll find

plenty to choose from here. And, of course, there are scrumptious hot and cold desserts. These range from traditional Old English Trifle, Strawberry and Apple Crumble, and Apricot and Orange Jelly to more contemporary favourites, such as Boston Banoffee Pie, Floating Islands in Plum Sauce, and Raspberry Passion Fruit Swirls. So whether you are just browsing for ideas, or looking for something new to try, this superb collection of family recipes is certain to have the dish to fit the occasion.

Fish Soup

For extra flavour use some smoked fish in this soup and rub the bread with a garlic clove before toasting.

Serves 6

90ml/6 tbsp olive oil, plus extra to serve
1 onion, finely chopped
1 celery stick, chopped
1 carrot, chopped
60ml/4 tbsp chopped fresh flat leaf parsley
175ml/6fl oz/³⁄₄ cup dry white wine
3 tomatoes, peeled and chopped
2 garlic cloves, finely chopped
1.5 litres/2¹⁄₂ pints/6¹⁄₄ cups boiling water
900g/2¹⁄₄lb mixed fish fillets such as coley (pollock), rock salmon (huss), whiting, red mullet, red snapper or cod
salt and ground black pepper
French bread and grated cheese, to garnish

1 Heat the oil in a large pan over low heat. Add the onion and cook, stirring occasionally, for about 5 minutes, until just softened but not coloured.

2 Stir in the celery and carrot and cook, stirring occasionally for a further 5 minutes. Add the parsley.

3 Pour in the wine, increase the heat to medium and cook until it has reduced by about half. Stir in the tomatoes and garlic and cook, stirring occasionally, for 3–4 minutes. Pour in the boiling water and bring back to the boil, then lower the heat and simmer for 15 minutes.

4 Add the fish fillets and simmer for 10–15 minutes, or until they are tender. Season to taste with salt and pepper.

5 Remove the fish from the soup with a slotted spoon. Discard the skin and any bones, then place the flesh in a food processor with the rest of the soup and process until smooth. Taste again for seasoning. If the soup is too thick, add a little more water.

6 To serve, heat the soup to simmering and ladle into soup plates. Toast slices of bread and sprinkle with olive oil. Place two or three in each bowl and top with the grated cheese.

Smoked Haddock & Potato Soup

This Scottish soup's traditional name is "cullen skink". A "cullen" is a town's port district and "skink" means stock or broth.

Serves 6

350g/12oz finnan haddock (smoked haddock)
1 onion, chopped
1 bouquet garni
900ml/1¹⁄₂ pints/3³⁄₄ cups water
500g/1¹⁄₄lb potatoes, quartered
600ml/1 pint/2¹⁄₂ cups milk
40g/1¹⁄₂oz/3 tbsp butter
salt and ground black pepper
chopped fresh chives, to garnish
crusty bread, to serve (optional)

1 Put the haddock, onion, bouquet garni and measured water into a large pan and bring to the boil. Skim the scum from the surface, then cover the pan with a tight-fitting lid. Lower the heat and poach gently for 10–15 minutes, or until the haddock flakes easily.

2 Remove the poached fish from the pan using a fish slice or slotted spatula and remove the skin and bones. Flake the flesh and reserve. Return the skin and bones to the pan and simmer, uncovered, for 30 minutes.

3 Strain the fish stock and return to the rinsed-out pan, then add the potatoes and simmer for about 25 minutes, or until tender. Remove the potatoes from the pan using a slotted spoon. Add the milk to the pan and bring to the boil.

4 Meanwhile, mash the potatoes with the butter, then whisk into the milk in the pan until thick and creamy. Add the flaked fish to the pan and adjust the seasoning. Sprinkle with chopped chives, ladle into warmed soup bowls and serve immediately with crusty bread, if you like.

Cook's Tip
Try to find traditionally smoked fish, which is quite a pale colour, rather than chemically processed haddock, which has been dyed a bright yellow.

Fish Energy 255kcal/1064kJ; Protein 28.1g; Carbohydrate 3.6g, of which sugars 3.3g; Fat 12.3g, of which saturates 1.8g; Cholesterol 69mg; Calcium 27mg; Fibre 1g; Sodium 102mg.
Haddock Energy 205kcal/864kJ; Protein 16.1g; Carbohydrate 19g, of which sugars 6.4g; Fat 7.8g, of which saturates 4.7g; Cholesterol 41mg; Calcium 137mg; Fibre 1g; Sodium 132mg.

Corn & Shellfish Chowder

"Chowder" comes from the French word *chaudron*, meaning a large pot in which the soup is cooked.

Serves 4

25g/1oz/2 tbsp butter
1 small onion, chopped
350g/12oz can corn, drained
600ml/1 pint/2 1/2 cups milk
2 spring onions (scallions), finely chopped
115g/4oz/1 cup peeled, cooked prawns (shrimp)
175g/6oz can white crab meat, drained and flaked
150ml/1/4 pint/2/3 cup single (light) cream
pinch of cayenne pepper
salt and ground black pepper
4 whole prawns in the shell, to garnish (optional)

1 Melt the butter in a large, heavy pan over medium heat. Add the onion and cook, stirring occasionally, for 4–5 minutes, until softened.

2 Reserve 30ml/2 tbsp of the corn for the garnish and add the remainder to the pan, then pour in the milk. Bring the soup to the boil, then reduce the heat to low, cover the pan with a tight-fitting lid and simmer gently for 5 minutes.

3 Ladle the soup into a blender or food processor, in batches if necessary, and process until smooth.

4 Return the soup to the rinsed-out pan and stir in the spring onions, prawns, crab meat, cream and cayenne pepper. Reheat gently over low heat, stirring occasionally. Do not let the soup come to the boil.

5 Meanwhile, place the reserved corn kernels in a small frying pan without oil and dry-fry over a medium heat until golden and toasted.

6 When the soup is hot, season to taste with salt and pepper and ladle it into warmed soup bowls. Garnish each bowl with a sprinkling of the toasted corn kernels and a whole prawn, if using, and serve immediately.

Thai-style Corn Soup

This is a very quick and easy soup. If you are using frozen prawns, thaw them before adding to the soup.

Serves 4

2.5ml/1/2 tsp sesame or sunflower oil
2 spring onions (scallions), thinly sliced
1 garlic clove, crushed
600ml/1 pint/2 1/2 cups chicken stock
425g/15oz can cream-style corn
225g/8oz/2 cups cooked, peeled prawns (shrimp)
5ml/1 tsp green chilli paste or chilli sauce (optional)
salt and ground black pepper
fresh coriander (cilantro) or parsley leaves, to garnish

1 Heat the oil in a large, heavy pan over medium heat. Add the spring onions and garlic and cook for about 1 minute, until softened but not browned.

2 Stir in the chicken stock, cream-style corn, prawns and chilli paste or sauce, if using. Bring the soup just to the boil, stirring occasionally, then remove the pan from the heat.

3 Season the soup to taste with salt and pepper, ladle it into warmed soup bowls, sprinkle with fresh coriander or parsley leaves to garnish and serve immediately.

Variations
• *For a Chinese version of this soup add 5ml/1 tsp grated fresh root ginger to the pan with the spring onions (scallions) and garlic in step 1 and substitute finely shredded, cooked chicken for the prawns (shrimp) in step 2. Garnish the soup with rings of spring onion, using the green part only.*
• *For a more pungent version add 10ml/2 tsp grated galangal or fresh root ginger and 1 lemon grass stalk, cut into 2.5cm/1in lengths, to the pan with the spring onions and garlic in step 1. Remove and discard the pieces of lemon grass before ladling the soup into bowls. Serve with a sweet chilli sauce or a chilli relish handed separately.*

Chowder Energy 359kcal/1506kJ; Protein 22.2g; Carbohydrate 32.5g, of which sugars 17.3g; Fat 16.5g, of which saturates 9.7g; Cholesterol 130mg; Calcium 299mg; Fibre 1.5g; Sodium 646mg.
Corn Soup Energy 177kcal/751kJ; Protein 13.1g; Carbohydrate 28.4g, of which sugars 10.4g; Fat 2g, of which saturates 0.3g; Cholesterol 110mg; Calcium 51mg; Fibre 1.6g; Sodium 394mg.

Haddock & Broccoli Chowder

This hearty soup makes a meal in itself when served with crusty bread.

Serves 4
4 spring onions (scallions), sliced
450g/1lb new potatoes, diced
300ml/½ pint/1¼ cups fish
    stock
300ml/½ pint/1¼ cups milk
1 bay leaf
225g/8oz/2 cups broccoli
    florets, sliced
450g/1lb smoked haddock
    fillets, skinned
200g/7oz can corn, drained
ground black pepper
chopped spring onions, to garnish

1 Place the spring onions and potatoes in a pan and add the stock, milk and bay leaf. Bring to the boil, reduce the heat, cover and simmer for 10 minutes.

2 Add the broccoli. Cut the fish into bitesize chunks and add to the pan with the corn. Season with pepper, then cover again and simmer until the fish is cooked through.

3 Remove and discard the bay leaf, sprinkle the chopped spring onions over the soup and serve immediately.

Cock-a-leekie Soup

This healthy main course soup has a sweet touch.

Serves 4–6
1.5kg/3lb chicken
1 bouquet garni
4 leeks, thickly sliced
8–12 ready-to-eat prunes
salt and pepper

1 Simmer the chicken in a covered pan with 1.2 litres/2 pints/ 5 cups water and the bouquet garni for 40 minutes. Add the leeks and prunes and simmer for a further 20 minutes.

2 Discard the bouquet garni. Remove the chicken, discard the skin and bones and chop the flesh. Return the chicken to the pan and season to taste. Reheat the soup and serve.

Split Pea & Bacon Soup

This soup is also called "London Particular", named after the notorious city fogs of the nineteenth century. The fogs, in turn,. were named "pea-soupers".

Serves 4
15g/½ oz/1 tbsp butter
115g/4oz/⅔ cup chopped smoked
    lean back bacon
1 large onion, chopped
1 carrot, chopped
1 celery stick, chopped
75g/3oz/scant ½ cup split peas
1.2 litres/2 pints/5 cups chicken
    stock
2 thick slices firm bread, buttered
    and with crusts removed
2 rashers (strips) streaky
    (fatty) bacon
salt and ground black pepper

1 Melt the butter in a pan over medium heat. Add the back bacon and cook until the fat runs. Stir in the onion, carrot and celery and cook for 2–3 minutes.

2 Add the split peas, followed by the stock. Bring to the boil, stirring occasionally, then lower the heat, cover with a tight-fitting lid and simmer for 45–60 minutes.

3 Meanwhile, preheat the oven to 180°C/350°F/Gas 4. Place the bread on a baking sheet and bake for about 20 minutes, until crisp and brown, then cut into dice.

4 Grill (broil) the streaky bacon under a preheated grill (broiler) until very crisp, then chop finely.

5 When the soup is ready, season to taste and ladle into warmed soup bowls. Sprinkle each serving with the chopped bacon and croûtons and serve immediately.

> **Cook's Tip**
> For additional flavour you could spread the bread with herb or garlic butter before baking in the oven. Alternatively, you could sprinkle the bread slices with freshly grated Parmesan cheese and bake until it is golden and bubbling.

Haddock Energy 276kcal/1172kJ; Protein 30g; Carbohydrate 36g, of which sugars 10.7g; Fat 2.4g, of which saturates 0.6g; Cholesterol 43mg; Calcium 161mg; Fibre 3.5g; Sodium 1041mg.
Cock-a-leekie Energy 281kcal/1189kJ; Protein 24g; Carbohydrate 39.8g, of which sugars 38.4g; Fat 3.9g, of which saturates 0.9g; Cholesterol 92mg; Calcium 88mg; Fibre 10.1g; Sodium 94mg.
Pea & Bacon Energy 171kcal/710kJ; Protein 8.3g; Carbohydrate 9.9g, of which sugars 3.1g; Fat 11.2g, of which saturates 4.8g; Cholesterol 31mg; Calcium 31mg; Fibre 1.1g; Sodium 705mg.

Stuffed Mushrooms

These flavoursome mushrooms also make an excellent accompaniment to a main course.

Serves 4

25g/1oz/2 tbsp butter, plus extra
    for greasing and brushing
275g/10oz spinach,
    stalks removed
400g/14oz medium
    cap mushrooms
25g/1oz bacon, chopped
1/2 small onion, chopped
75g/5 tbsp double (heavy) cream
about 60ml/4 tbsp grated
    Cheddar or feta cheese
30ml/2 tbsp fresh breadcrumbs
salt and ground black pepperfresh
    parsley sprigs, to garnish

1 Preheat the oven to 190°C/375°F/Gas 5. Grease an ovenproof dish with butter. Wash but do not dry the spinach. Place it in a pan, cover and cook, stirring occasionally, for 4–5 minutes, until just wilted.

2 Place the spinach in a colander and squeeze out as much liquid as possible, then chop finely. Snap the stalks from the mushrooms and chop the stalks finely.

3 Melt the butter in a pan. Add the bacon, onion and mushroom stalks and cook for about 5 minutes. Stir in the spinach, cook for a few seconds, then remove the pan from the heat. Stir in the cream and season to taste with salt and pepper.

4 Brush the mushroom caps with melted butter, then place, gills uppermost, in a single layer in the prepared dish.

5 Divide the spinach mixture among the mushrooms. Mix together the cheese and breadcrumbs and sprinkle over the mushrooms, then bake for about 20 minutes until the mushrooms are tender. Serve warm, garnished with parsley.

Cook's Tip
Squeeze out all the excess water from the cooked spinach, otherwise the stuffing will be too soggy.

Mulligatawny Soup

Choose red split lentils for the best colour, although green or brown lentils could also be used.

Serves 4

50g/2oz/4 tbsp butter or 60ml/
    4 tbsp vegetable oil
2 large chicken pieces (about
    350g/12oz each)
1 onion, chopped
1 carrot, chopped
1 small turnip, chopped
about 15ml/1 tbsp curry powder,
    to taste
4 cloves
6 black peppercorns,
    lightly crushed
50g/2oz/1/4 cup lentils
900ml/1 1/2 pints/3 3/4 cups
    chicken stock
40g/1 1/2oz/1/4 cup sultanas
    (golden raisins)
salt and ground black pepper

1 Heat the butter or oil in a large pan over medium-high heat. Add the chicken and cook, turning occasionally, for about 10 minutes, until golden brown all over. Using tongs, transfer the chicken to a plate.

2 Lower the heat, add the onion, carrot and turnip and cook, stirring occasionally, for about 10 minutes, until softened and lightly coloured. Stir in the curry powder, cloves and peppercorns and cook for 1–2 minutes, then add the lentils.

3 Pour the stock into the pan, bring to the boil, then add the sultanas. Return the chicken to the pan together with any juices from the plate. Lower the heat, cover and simmer gently for about 1 1/4 hours.

4 Remove the chicken from the pan and discard the skin and bones. Chop the flesh into bitesize chunks, return to the soup and reheat. Season to taste with salt and pepper. Ladle the soup into warmed soup plates and serve immediately.

Cook's Tip
Use a good quality curry powder, which will add subtle flavour as well as heat to this spicy soup.

Mulligatawny Energy 513kcal/2136kJ; Protein 35.8g; Carbohydrate 17.3g, of which sugars 10.1g; Fat 33.9g, of which saturates 12.9g; Cholesterol 219mg; Calcium 42mg; Fibre 1.8g; Sodium 229mg.
Mushrooms Energy 281kcal/1166kJ; Protein 9.9g; Carbohydrate 8.9g, of which sugars 2.7g; Fat 22.8g, of which saturates 13.5g; Cholesterol 58mg; Calcium 258mg; Fibre 2.9g; Sodium 388mg.

Leek Terrine with Deli Meats

This attractive appetizer is surprisingly simple yet looks really spectacular. For best results it should be made a day ahead.

Serves 6
20–24 small young leeks
about 225g/8oz mixed sliced
    meats, such as prosciutto,
    coppa and pancetta
50g/2oz/½ cup walnuts, toasted
    and chopped
salt and ground black pepper

For the dressing
60ml/4 tbsp walnut oil
60ml/4 tbsp olive oil
30ml/2 tbsp white wine vinegar
5ml/1 tsp wholegrain mustard

1 Cut off the roots and most of the green part from the leeks. Wash them thoroughly under cold running water.

2 Bring a large pan of salted water to the boil. Add the leeks, bring the water back to the boil, then simmer for 6–8 minutes, until the leeks are just tender. Drain well.

3 Fill a 450g/1lb loaf tin (pan) with the leeks, placing them alternately head to tail and sprinkling each layer as you go with salt and pepper.

4 Put another loaf tin inside the first and gently press down on the leeks. Carefully invert both tins and let any water drain out.

5 Place one or two weights on top of the tins and chill the terrine for at least 4 hours or overnight.

6 To make the dressing, whisk together the walnut and olive oils, vinegar and mustard in a small bowl. Season to taste.

7 Carefully turn out the terrine on to a board and cut into slices using a large, sharp knife. Lay the slices of leek terrine on serving plates and arrange the slices of meat beside them.

8 Spoon the dressing over the slices of terrine and sprinkle the chopped walnuts over the top. Serve immediately.

Garlic Prawns in Filo Tartlets

Tartlets made with crisp layers of filo pastry and filled with garlic prawns make a tempting, attractive and unusual appetizer.

Serves 4
For the tartlets
50g/2oz/4 tbsp butter, melted
2–3 large sheets filo pastry

For the filling
115g/4oz/½ cup butter
2–3 garlic cloves, crushed
1 fresh red chilli, seeded
    and chopped
350g/12oz/3 cups peeled,
    cooked prawns (shrimp)
30ml/2 tbsp chopped fresh
    parsley or chives
salt and ground black pepper

1 Preheat the oven to 200°C/400°F/Gas 6. Brush four individual 7.5cm/3in flan tins (pans) with melted butter.

2 Cut the filo pastry into twelve 10cm/4in squares and brush with the melted butter.

3 Place three squares of pastry inside each tin, overlapping them at slight angles and carefully frilling the edges and points while forming a good hollow in each centre. Bake the pastry for 10–15 minutes, until crisp and golden. Cool slightly and remove from the tins.

4 To make the filling, melt the butter in a large frying pan over medium-low heat. Add the garlic, chilli and prawns and cook, stirring frequently, for 1–2 minutes to warm through. Stir in the parsley or chives and season to taste with salt and pepper.

5 Using a spoon, divide the prawn filling among the tartlets and serve immediately.

Cook's Tips
• If using frozen filo pastry, leave it to thaw thoroughly first but keep it covered to prevent it from drying out.
• If using fresh filo pastry rather than frozen, wrap and freeze any leftover sheets for future use.

Terrine Energy 232kcal/962kJ; Protein 10.5g; Carbohydrate 3.3g, of which sugars 2.6g; Fat 19.7g, of which saturates 2.4g; Cholesterol 22mg; Calcium 37mg; Fibre 2.4g; Sodium 453mg.
Tartlets Energy 440kcal/1825kJ; Protein 17.6g; Carbohydrate 15g, of which sugars 0.7g; Fat 34.8g, of which saturates 21.6g; Cholesterol 259mg; Calcium 118mg; Fibre 1g; Sodium 419mg.

Smoked Salmon & Dill Blinis

Blinis, small pancakes of Russian origin, are so easy to make, yet they make a sophisticated dinner party appetizer and great canapés.

Serves 4
115g/4oz/1 cup buckwheat flour
115g/4oz/1 cup plain (all-purpose) flour
pinch of salt
15ml/1 tbsp easy-blend (rapid-rise) dried yeast
2 eggs
350ml/12fl oz/1 ½ cups warm milk
15ml/1 tbsp melted butter, plus extra for pan-frying
150ml/¼ pint/⅔ cup crème fraîche or sour cream
45ml/3 tbsp chopped fresh dill
225g/8oz smoked salmon, thinly sliced
fresh dill sprigs, to garnish

1 Mix together the buckwheat and plain flours in a large bowl with the salt. Sprinkle in the yeast and mix well. Separate one of the eggs. Whisk together the whole egg and the yolk, the warm milk and the melted butter.

2 Pour the egg mixture on to the flour mixture. Beat well to form a smooth batter. Cover with clear film (plastic wrap) and leave to rise in a warm place for 1–2 hours.

3 Whisk the remaining egg white in a large, grease-free bowl until stiff peaks form, then gently fold into the batter.

4 Preheat a heavy frying pan or griddle and brush with melted butter. Drop tablespoons of the batter on to the pan, spacing them well apart. Cook for about 40 seconds, until bubbles appear on the surface.

5 Flip over the blinis and cook for 30 seconds on the other side. Wrap in foil and keep warm in a low oven. Repeat with the remaining mixture, buttering the pan each time.

6 Combine the crème fraîche or sour cream and chopped dill. Top the blinis with slices of smoked salmon and a spoonful of dill cream. Garnish with dill sprigs and serve immediately.

Egg & Tomato Salad with Crab

13

You could also adjust the quantities in this tasty salad to make a quick, light and healthy weekday meal.

Serves 4
1 round (butterhead) lettuce
2 x 200g/7oz cans crab meat, drained
4 hard-boiled eggs, sliced
16 cherry tomatoes, halved
½ green (bell) pepper, seeded and thinly sliced
6 pitted black olives, sliced

For the dressing
45ml/3 tbsp chilli sauce
250g/8fl oz/1 cup mayonnaise
10ml/2 tsp freshly squeezed lemon juice
½ green pepper, seeded and finely chopped
5ml/1 tsp prepared horseradish
5ml/1 tsp Worcestershire sauce

1 First make the dressing. Place all the ingredients in a bowl and mix well with a balloon whisk. Cover with clear film (plastic wrap) and set aside in a cool place until required.

2 Line four plates with the lettuce leaves. Divide the crab meat among them, mounding it up in the centre of each plate. Arrange the slices of egg around the outside with the tomato halves on top.

3 Spoon a little of the dressing over the crab meat. Arrange the green pepper slices on top and sprinkle with the olives. Serve immediately with the remaining dressing handed separately.

Variations
• Use freshly cooked or thawed frozen crab meat instead of canned.
• Substitute well-drained, canned tuna for the crab meat.
• Use peeled cooked prawns (shrimp) instead of crab meat, but try to avoid frozen ones as the texture can be woolly.
• Use 16 whole quail's eggs, boiled for 1½ minutes, then cooled and shelled, instead of sliced hard-boiled eggs.

Blinis Energy 557kcal/2328kJ; Protein 26.3g; Carbohydrate 51.8g, of which sugars 5.5g; Fat 28.8g, of which saturates 16.3g; Cholesterol 178mg; Calcium 197mg; Fibre 1.5g; Sodium 1185mg.
Salad Energy 608kcal/2515kJ; Protein 25.9g; Carbohydrate 4.8g, of which sugars 4.5g; Fat 54.2g, of which saturates 9g; Cholesterol 309mg; Calcium 171mg; Fibre 1.3g; Sodium 1018mg.

Aubergine & Red Pepper Pâté

This simple pâté of baked aubergine, pink peppercorns and red peppers has more than a hint of garlic.

Serves 4

3 aubergines (eggplants)
2 large red (bell) peppers
5 garlic cloves, unpeeled
7.5ml/1½ tsp pink peppercorns in brine, drained and crushed
30ml/2 tbsp chopped fresh coriander (cilantro)
mixed salad leaves, to serve

1 Preheat the oven to 200°C/400°F/Gas 6. Arrange the whole aubergines, peppers and garlic cloves on a baking sheet and bake for 10 minutes. Transfer the garlic cloves to a chopping board. Turn over the aubergines and peppers and return them to the oven for a further 20 minutes.

2 Meanwhile, peel the garlic cloves and place them in a blender or food processor.

3 When the peppers are blistered and charred, use tongs to transfer them to a plastic bag, tie the top and leave to cool. Return the aubergines to the oven for a further 10 minutes.

4 Remove the aubergines from the oven. Split them in half and scoop the flesh into a sieve (strainer) placed over a bowl. Press the flesh with a spoon to remove the bitter juices.

5 Add the aubergine flesh to the garlic and process until smooth. Place in a large mixing bowl.

6 Peel and seed the red peppers and chop the flesh. Stir it into the aubergine mixture. Mix in the pink peppercorns and chopped fresh coriander and serve immediately on a bed of mixed salad leaves.

> **Cook's Tip**
> Serve the pâté with Melba toast, oatcakes, fingers of olive focaccia or mini pitta breads.

Red Pepper Watercress Parcels

The peppery watercress flavour contrasts delightfully with sweet red pepper in these crisp filo parcels.

Makes 8

3 red (bell) peppers
175g/6oz watercress or rocket (arugula)
225g/8oz 1 cup ricotta cheese
50g/2oz/½ cup toasted, chopped almonds
8 sheets filo pastry, thawed if frozen
30ml/2 tbsp olive oil
salt and ground black pepper

1 Preheat the oven to 190°C/375°F/Gas 5 and preheat the grill (broiler). Place the red peppers on a baking sheet and grill (broil), turning occasionally with tongs, until blistered and charred. Use tongs to transfer to a plastic bag, tie the top and leave to cool.

2 When the peppers are cool enough to handle, peel and seed them. Pat dry with kitchen paper.

3 Place the peppers and watercress or rocket in a food processor and pulse until coarsely chopped. Spoon the mixture into a bowl. Stir in the ricotta and almonds and season to taste with salt and pepper.

4 Working with one sheet of filo pastry at a time and keeping the others covered, cut out two 18cm/7in and two 5cm/2in squares from each sheet. Brush one large square with a little olive oil and place a second large square at an angle of 45 degrees to form a star shape.

5 Place one of the smaller squares in the centre of the star shape, brush lightly with olive oil and top with the second small square.

6 Top with one-eighth of the red pepper mixture. Bring the edges together to form a purse shape and twist to seal. Place on a lightly greased baking sheet and cook for 25–30 minutes, until golden. Serve immediately.

Pâté Energy 51kcal/213kJ; Protein 2.2g; Carbohydrate 8.9g, of which sugars 8.4g; Fat 1g, of which saturates 0.2g; Cholesterol 0mg; Calcium 22mg; Fibre 4.4g; Sodium 7mg.
Parcels Energy 163kcal/677kJ; Protein 5.9g; Carbohydrate 10.9g, of which sugars 5.7g; Fat 10.9g, of which saturates 3.4g; Cholesterol 12mg; Calcium 67mg; Fibre 2.1g; Sodium 15mg.

Nutty Cheese Balls

An extremely quick and simple recipe. Try making smaller portions to serve as canapés at a drinks party.

Serves 4

225g/8oz/1 cup low-fat soft
 (farmer's) cheese
50g/2oz/¹/₂ cup Dolcelatte or
 Gorgonzola cheese
15ml/1 tbsp finely chopped onion
15ml/1 tbsp finely chopped celery
15ml/1 tbsp finely chopped
 fresh parsley
15ml/1 tbsp finely
 chopped gherkin
5ml/1 tsp brandy or
 port (optional)
pinch of paprika
50g/2oz/¹/₂ cup walnuts,
 coarsely chopped
90ml/6 tbsp chopped fresh chives
salt and ground black pepper

To serve

crusty bread
mixed salad leaves
sliced radishes

1 Put the soft cheese and Dolcelatte or Gorgonzola in a bowl and beat with a spoon until combined and quite smooth.

2 Add the onion, celery, parsley, gherkin, brandy or port, if using, paprika and walnuts, season with salt and pepper and stir well to combine.

3 Divide the mixture into 12 pieces and roll each piece into a ball between the palms of your hands.

4 Roll each ball gently in the chopped chives and place on a plate. Cover with clear film (plastic wrap) or foil, and chill in the refrigerator for about 1 hour. Serve with crusty bread, mixed salad leaves and sliced radishes.

> **Variation**
> For an alternative look, mix the chives with the rest of the ingredients in step 2 but omit the walnuts. Instead, chop the walnuts very finely and use to coat the cheese balls in step 4. For a larger number of guests make one batch of each type and serve a mixture of the two.

Fried Tomatoes with Polenta Crust

This recipe works well with green tomatoes freshly picked from the garden or greenhouse.

Serves 4

4 large firm under-ripe tomatoes
115g/4oz/scant 1 cup polenta or
 coarse cornmeal
5ml/1 tsp dried oregano
 or marjoram
2.5ml/¹/₂ tsp garlic powder
1 egg
plain (all-purpose) flour,
 for dredging
vegetable oil, for deep-frying
salt and ground black pepper
salad, to serve

1 Cut the tomatoes into thick slices. Mix the polenta or cornmeal with the oregano or marjoram and garlic powder in a shallow bowl.

2 Lightly beat the egg in another shallow bowl and season with salt and pepper. Put the flour in a third shallow bowl. Dip the tomato slices first into the flour, then into the egg and finally into the polenta or cornmeal mixture.

3 Fill a shallow frying pan one-third full of vegetable oil and heat steadily until quite hot.

4 Slip the tomato slices into the oil carefully, a few at a time, and fry on each side until crisp. Remove with a slotted spoon and drain well on kitchen paper. Repeat with the remaining tomatoes, reheating the oil in between each batch. Serve immediately with salad.

> **Variations**
> • This is also a tasty way to cook mushrooms. Coat 450g/1lb whole button (white) mushrooms with flour, seasoned egg and the polenta mixture and deep-fry until crisp.
> • Substitute goat's cheese or mozzarella for the tomatoes. Cut 225–275g/8–10oz cheese into fairly thick slices, then coat and cook as in the recipe. Bocconcini, bitesize balls of mozzarella, would be perfect for this treatment.

Cheese Balls Energy 213kcal/883kJ; Protein 13.4g; Carbohydrate 4g, of which sugars 3.5g; Fat 16.9g, of which saturates 6g; Cholesterol 23mg; Calcium 170mg; Fibre 1.4g; Sodium 409mg.
Tomatoes Energy 215kcal/897kJ; Protein 5g; Carbohydrate 24.1g, of which sugars 3.1g; Fat 10.9g, of which saturates 1.5g; Cholesterol 48mg; Calcium 15mg; Fibre 1.6g; Sodium 27mg.

English Ploughman's Pâté

This is a contemporary interpretation of the traditional ploughman's lunch – bread, cheese and a variety of pickles.

Serves 4
50g/2oz/3 tbsp full-fat
soft (farmer's) cheese
50g/2oz/½ cup grated Caerphilly
or other crumbly white cheese
50g/2oz/½ cup grated Double
Gloucester or other mellow,
semi-hard cheese

4 pickled silverskin onions,
drained and finely chopped
15ml/1 tbsp apricot chutney
30ml/2 tbsp butter, melted
30ml/2 tbsp chopped fresh chives
4 slices soft-grain bread
salt and ground black pepper
watercress or rocket (arugula) and
cherry tomatoes, to serve

1 Mix together the soft cheese, grated cheeses, pickled onions, chutney and butter in a bowl and season lightly with salt and ground black pepper.

2 Spoon the mixture on to a sheet of greaseproof (waxed) paper and roll up into a cylinder, smoothing the mixture into a roll with your hands. Scrunch the ends of the paper together and twist them to seal. Place in the freezer for about 30 minutes, until the roll is just firm.

3 Spread the chives on a plate, then unwrap the chilled cheese pâté. Roll it in the chives until evenly coated. Wrap in clear film (plastic wrap) and chill for 10 minutes in the refrigerator.

4 Preheat the grill (broiler). Lightly toast the bread on both sides. Cut off the crusts and slice each piece in half horizontally to make two very thin slices. Cut each half into two triangles. Grill (broil) again, untoasted side up, until golden and curled at the edges.

5 Slice the pâté into rounds with a sharp knife and serve three or four rounds per person with the toast, watercress or rocket and cherry tomatoes.

Golden Cheese Puffs

Serve these deep-fried puffs – called *aigrettes* in France – with a fruity chutney and a green salad.

Makes 8
50g/2oz/½ cup plain (all-
purpose) flour
15g/½oz/1 tbsp butter
1 egg
1 egg yolk

50g/2oz/½ cup finely grated
mature (sharp) Cheddar cheese
15ml/1 tbsp freshly grated
Parmesan cheese
2.5ml/½ tsp mustard powder
pinch of cayenne pepper
vegetable oil, for deep-frying
salt and ground black pepper
mango chutney and green salad,
to serve

1 Sift the flour on to a square of greaseproof (waxed) paper and set aside. Place the butter and 150ml/⅔ pint/⅔ cup water in a pan and heat gently until the butter has melted.

2 Bring the liquid to the boil and tip in the flour all at once. Remove the pan from the heat and stir well with a wooden spoon until the mixture begins to leave the sides of the pan and forms a ball. Leave to cool slightly.

3 Beat the egg and egg yolk together in a bowl with a fork and then gradually add to the mixture in the pan, beating well after each addition.

4 Stir the Cheddar and Parmesan cheeses, mustard powder and cayenne pepper into the mixture and season to taste with salt and pepper.

5 Heat the vegetable oil in a deep-fryer or large, heavy pan to 190°C/375°F, or until a cube of day-old bread browns in 30 seconds. Drop four spoonfuls of the cheese mixture into the oil at a time and deep-fry for 2–3 minutes, until golden. Remove with a slotted spoon, drain on kitchen paper and keep hot in the oven while cooking the remaining mixture.

6 Serve two puffs per person with a spoonful of mango chutney and green salad.

Pâté Energy 288kcal/1200kJ; Protein 10.6g; Carbohydrate 18.7g, of which sugars 5.1g; Fat 19g, of which saturates 11.9g; Cholesterol 52mg; Calcium 267mg; Fibre 1.3g; Sodium 511mg.
Cheese Puffs Energy 162kcal/669kJ; Protein 3.5g; Carbohydrate 5.8g, of which sugars 0g; Fat 13.9g, of which saturates 4.1g; Cholesterol 61mg; Calcium 77mg; Fibre 0g; Sodium 90mg.

Tricolor Salad

This can be a simple appetizer if served on individual salad plates, or part of a light buffet meal laid out on a platter.

Serves 4–6

1 small red onion, thinly sliced
6 large full-flavoured tomatoes
extra virgin olive oil, to drizzle
50g/2oz rocket (arugula) or watercress, chopped
175g/6oz mozzarella cheese, thinly sliced
salt and ground black pepper
30ml/2 tbsp pine nuts, to garnish (optional)

1 Soak the onion slices in a bowl of cold water for about 30 minutes, then drain and pat dry with kitchen paper.

2 Cut a cross in the tops of the tomatoes, place in a heatproof bowl and pour boiling water over them. Leave for 1 minute, then drain and peel off the skins. Remove the cores and slice the flesh. Arrange half the sliced tomatoes on a large platter or divide them among small plates.

3 Drizzle liberally with olive oil, then layer with half the chopped rocket or watercress and half the soaked onion slices, seasoning well with salt and pepper. Add half the mozzarella, then drizzle with more olive oil and season again.

4 Repeat with the remaining tomato slices, salad leaves, onion slices, mozzarella and olive oil.

5 Season well to finish and complete with some olive oil and a good sprinkling of pine nuts, if using. Cover the salad with clear film (plastic wrap) and chill in the refrigerator for at least 2 hours before serving.

> **Cook's Tip**
> When lightly salted, tomatoes make their own dressing with their natural juices. The sharpness of the rocket (arugula) or watercress offsets them wonderfully.

Minted Melon Salad

Use two different varieties of melon in this salad, such as Charentais and Galia or Ogen.

Serves 4

2 ripe melons
fresh mint sprigs, to garnish

For the dressing
30ml/2 tbsp coarsely chopped fresh mint
5ml/1 tsp caster (superfine) sugar
30ml/2 tbsp raspberry vinegar
90ml/6 tbsp extra virgin olive oil
salt and ground black pepper

1 Halve the melons, then scoop out the seeds using a dessertspoon. Cut the melons into thin wedges using a large sharp knife and remove the skins.

2 Arrange the two different varieties of melon wedges alternately among four individual serving plates.

3 To make the dressing, whisk together the mint, sugar, vinegar and olive oil in a small bowl and season to taste with salt and pepper. Alternatively, put them in a screw-top jar, close the lid and shake well until combined.

4 Spoon the mint dressing over the melon wedges and garnish with mint sprigs. Chill in the refrigerator for about 15 minutes before serving.

> **Cook's Tip**
> You can make raspberry vinegar yourself by steeping the fresh fruit in wine vinegar and then straining it. Steeping another batch of fruit in the same vinegar intensifies the flavour.

> **Variation**
> You could also try an orange-fleshed Cantaloupe with a pale green Ogen, or choose a small white-fleshed Honeydew for a different variation.

Tricolor Energy 98kcal/408kJ; Protein 6.5g; Carbohydrate 4g, of which sugars 3.8g; Fat 6.3g, of which saturates 4.1g; Cholesterol 17mg; Calcium 129mg; Fibre 1.3g; Sodium 136mg.
Melon Energy 218kcal/904kJ; Protein 1.7g; Carbohydrate 15.7g, of which sugars 15.1g; Fat 16.8g, of which saturates 2.4g; Cholesterol 0mg; Calcium 59mg; Fibre 1g; Sodium 80mg.

Pear & Roquefort Salad

The partnership of blue cheese with sweet fruit and crunchy nuts is magical.

Serves 4
50g/2oz/½ cup hazelnuts
3 ripe pears
lemon juice
about 175g/6oz mixed fresh
    salad leaves

175g/6oz Roquefort cheese

For the dressing
30ml/2 tbsp hazelnut oil
45ml/3 tbsp olive oil
15ml/1 tbsp cider vinegar
5ml/1 tsp Dijon mustard
salt and ground black pepper

1 Toast the hazelnuts in a dry frying pan over low heat for about 2 minutes until golden, tossing frequently to prevent them from burning. Chop the nuts and set aside.

2 To make the dressing, mix together the oils, vinegar and mustard in a bowl or place in a screw-top jar and shake to combine. Season to taste with salt and pepper.

3 Peel, core and slice the pears, then toss them in the lemon juice to prevent them from discolouring.

4 Divide the salad leaves among four serving plates, then place the pears on top. Crumble the cheese and scatter over the salad along with the toasted hazelnuts. Spoon over the dressing and serve immediately.

Cook's Tip
Choose ripe but firm Comice or Williams' pears for this salad. Toss the pears, cheese and nuts with the leaves, if you prefer.

Variation
Replace the hazelnuts with walnuts, and use watercress instead of mixed salad – the peppery leaves go well with the pears.

Mediterranean Mixed Pepper Salad

This Italian-style salad is great to serve as part of a cold lunch spread, with salamis, hams and chunks of warm ciabatta bread.

Serves 4
2 red (bell) peppers, halved and
    seeded

2 yellow (bell) peppers, halved
    and seeded
150ml/¼ pint/⅔ cup olive oil
1 onion, thinly sliced
2 garlic cloves, crushed
generous squeeze of lemon juice
chopped fresh parsley, to garnish

1 Place the peppers, skin-side up, under a hot grill (broiler) and grill (broil) until beginning to char and blister. Put the pepper pieces in a bowl, cover with kitchen paper and leave to cool for 10 minutes.

2 Meanwhile, heat 30ml/2 tbsp of the olive oil in a frying pan and fry the onion for about 5–6 minutes over medium heat, stirring occasionally, until softened and translucent. Remove from the heat and reserve.

3 Remove the peppers from the bowl, then peel off and discard the skins. Slice each pepper half into fairly thin strips.

4 Place the peppers, cooked onion and any oil from the pan into a bowl. Add the crushed garlic and pour in the remaining olive oil. Add a generous squeeze of lemon juice and season to taste with salt and pepper. Mix well, cover and marinate for 2–3 hours, stirring the mixture once or twice.

5 Just before serving, garnish the pepper salad with chopped fresh parsley.

Variation
Add 4 peeled and halved tomatoes to the pepper and onion mixture. Use a red onion and finish off with a sprinkling of black olive halves and torn basil leaves.

Pear Energy 381kcal/1579kJ; Protein 11.4g; Carbohydrate 12.8g, of which sugars 12.5g; Fat 31.9g, of which saturates 10.3g; Cholesterol 33mg; Calcium 256mg; Fibre 3.7g; Sodium 539mg.
Mixed Pepper Energy 299kcal/1233kJ; Protein 2.9g; Carbohydrate 14.4g, of which sugars 11.7g; Fat 25.8g, of which saturates 3.8g; Cholesterol 0mg; Calcium 20mg; Fibre 3.5g; Sodium 8mg.

Fresh Spinach & Avocado Salad

Young, tender spinach leaves make a change from lettuce. They are delicious served with avocado, cherry tomatoes and radishes in an unusual tofu sauce.

Serves 4–6

1 large avocado
juice of 1 lime
225g/8oz/4 cups baby spinach
    leaves
115g/4oz cherry tomatoes
4 spring onions (scallions), sliced
1/2 cucumber
50g/2oz radishes, sliced

For the dressing

115g/4oz soft silken tofu
45ml/3 tbsp milk
10ml/2 tsp mustard
2.5ml/1/2 tsp white wine vinegar
cayenne pepper
salt and ground black pepper
radish roses and fresh herb sprigs,
    to garnish

1 Cut the avocado in half, remove the stone and strip off the skin. Cut the flesh into slices. Transfer to a plate, drizzle over the lime juice and set aside.

2 Rinse and thoroughly dry the baby spinach leaves. Put them in a mixing bowl.

3 Cut the larger cherry tomatoes in half and add all the tomatoes to the mixing bowl with the spring onions. Cut the cucumber into even-size chunks and add to the bowl with the sliced radishes.

4 To make the dressing, put the silken tofu, milk, mustard, wine vinegar and a pinch of cayenne in a food processor or blender. Add salt and pepper to taste, then process for 30 seconds until the dressing is smooth.

5 Scrape the dressing into a bowl and add a little extra milk if you like a thinner consistency. Sprinkle with a little extra cayenne, garnish with radish roses and herb sprigs.

6 Arrange the avocado slices with the spinach salad on a serving dish and serve immediately, with the tofu dressing handed round separately.

Pear & Pecan Nut Salad

Toasted pecan nuts have a special affinity with crisp white pears. Their robust flavours combine well with a rich Blue Cheese and Chive dressing to make this a salad to remember.

Serves 4

75g/3oz/1/2 cup shelled pecan
    nuts, roughly chopped
3 crisp pears
175g/6oz/3 cups young spinach,
    stems removed
1 escarole or round (butterhead)
    lettuce
1 radicchio
salt and ground black pepper
crusty bread, to serve

1 Toast the pecan nuts under a medium grill (broiler) to bring out their flavour.

2 Cut the pears into quarters and remove the cores, but leave the skins intact. Cut into even slices.

3 Place the spinach, lettuce and radicchio leaves in a large bowl. Add the sliced pears and toasted pecans, then pour over the dressing and toss well.

4 Divide the salad among four plates and season with salt and pepper. Serve the salad with warm crusty bread.

Cook's Tip

• The pecan nuts will burn very quickly under the grill, so keep constant watch over them and remove them as soon as they change colour.
• To make 350ml/12 fl oz/1½ cups of Blue Cheese and Chive Dressing: remove the rind from 75g/3 oz blue cheese (Stilton, Bleu d'Auvergne or Gorgonzola) and combine with a third of 150ml/¼ pint/⅔ cup natural (plain) yogurt. Then add the remaining yogurt, 45ml/3 tbsp of olive oil and 30ml/1 tbsp lemon juice. and mix well. Stir in 15ml/1 tbsp chopped chives and season to taste with ground black pepper.

Spinach Energy 71kcal/293kJ; Protein 2.8g; Carbohydrate 2g, of which sugars 1.6g; Fat 5.7g, of which saturates 1.2g; Cholesterol 0mg; Calcium 135mg; Fibre 1.7g; Sodium 46mg.
Pear Energy 227kcal/939kJ; Protein 3.9g; Carbohydrate 14.6g, of which sugars 14.2g; Fat 17.3g, of which saturates 1.2g; Cholesterol 3mg; Calcium 117mg; Fibre 4.7g; Sodium 150mg.

Frankfurter Salad

A last-minute salad you can throw together using store-cupboard ingredients.

Serves 4
675g/1½ lb new potatoes
2 eggs
350g/12oz frankfurters
1 round (butterhead) lettuce, leaves separated
225g/8oz young spinach
30–45ml/2–3 tbsp oil and vinegar dressing
salt and ground black pepper

1 Boil the new potatoes in lightly salted water for 20 minutes. Drain, cover and keep warm.

2 Hard-boil the eggs for 12 minutes, then shell and quarter. Score the skins of the frankfurters cork-screw fashion, cover with boiling water and simmer for 5 minutes. Drain; keep warm.

3 Distribute the lettuce and spinach leaves among four plates, moisten the potatoes and frankfurters with dressing and arrange over the salad. Top with the eggs. Season with salt and pepper.

New Potato & Chive Salad

The secret is to add the dressing while the potatoes are still hot so that they absorb all the flavours.

Serves 4–6
675g/1½ lb new potatoes
45ml/3 tbsp olive oil
15ml/1 tbsp white wine vinegar
4ml/¾ tsp Dijon mustard
4 spring onions (scallions), finely chopped
175ml/6fl oz/¾ cup good quality mayonnaise
45ml/3 tbsp snipped fresh chives
salt and ground black pepper

1 Cook the potatoes, unpeeled, in boiling salted water until tender. Meanwhile, whisk together the oil, vinegar and mustard.

2 Drain the potatoes well, then immediately toss lightly with the vinegar mixture and spring onions and leave to cool. Stir in the mayonnaise and chives, season to taste and chill.

Watercress Potato Salad Bowl

New potatoes tossed with watercress, tomatoes and pumpkin seeds make a colourful, nutritious salad.

Serves 4
450g/1lb small new potatoes, unpeeled
1 bunch watercress
200g/7oz cherry tomatoes, halved
30ml/2 tbsp pumpkin seeds
45ml/3 tbsp low-fat fromage frais or natural (plain) yogurt
15ml/1 tbsp cider vinegar
5ml/1 tsp soft light brown sugar
salt and paprika

1 Cook the potatoes in lightly salted boiling water until just tender, then drain and leave to cool.

2 Toss together the potatoes, watercress, tomatoes and pumpkin seeds. Whisk together the fromage frais, vinegar, sugar, salt and paprika and, just before serving, toss with the salad.

Mixed Leafy Salad

This flavourful salad makes an ideal side dish for serving with meat and fish.

Serves 4
15g/1oz/½ cup mixed fresh herbs, such as chervil, tarragon (use sparingly), dill, basil, marjoram (use sparingly), flat leaf parsley, mint, sorrel, fennel and coriander (cilantro)
350g/12oz mixed salad leaves, such as rocket (arugula), radicchio, chicory (Belgian endive), watercress, frisée, baby spinach and oakleaf lettuce

For the dressing
50ml/2fl oz/¼ cup extra virgin olive oil
15ml/1 tbsp cider vinegar
salt and ground black pepper

1 Wash the herbs and salad leaves, then dry in a salad spinner, or use two clean, dry dish towels to pat them dry.

2 To make the dressing, blend together the olive oil and vinegar in a small bowl and season with salt and pepper to taste. Place all the leaves in a salad bowl. Toss with the dressing and serve.

Frankfurter Energy 472kcal/1969kJ; Protein 20g; Carbohydrate 30.9g, of which sugars 5g; Fat 29.3g, of which saturates 9.7g; Cholesterol 162mg; Calcium 146mg; Fibre 3.5g; Sodium 998mg.
Chive Salad Energy 334kcal/1385kJ; Protein 2.6g; Carbohydrate 19g, of which sugars 2.2g; Fat 28g, of which saturates 4.2g; Cholesterol 22mg; Calcium 27mg; Fibre 1.6g; Sodium 147mg.
Watercress Energy 152kcal/644kJ; Protein 6.1g; Carbohydrate 23.1g, of which sugars 5.2g; Fat 4.6g, of which saturates 0.7g; Cholesterol 0mg; Calcium 114mg; Fibre 2.8g; Sodium 45mg.
Mixed Leafy Salad Energy 92kcal/380kJ; Protein 0.8g; Carbohydrate 1.6g, of which sugars 1.6g; Fat 9.2g, of which saturates 1.4g; Cholesterol 0mg; Calcium 32mg; Fibre 1g; Sodium 4mg.

Parmesan & Poached Egg Salad

Soft poached eggs, hot croûtons and cool crisp salad leaves make a lively and unusual combination.

Serves 2

½ small loaf white bread
75ml/5 tbsp extra virgin olive oil
2 eggs
115g/4oz mixed salad leaves
2 garlic cloves, crushed
10ml/½ tbsp white wine vinegar
30ml/2 tbsp freshly shaved
    Parmesan cheese
ground black pepper

1 Remove the crust from the bread and discard it. Cut the bread into 2.5cm/1in cubes.

2 Heat 30ml/2 tbsp of the oil in a large frying pan. Add the bread cubes and cook for about 5 minutes, tossing the cubes occasionally, until they are crisp and golden brown all over.

3 Bring a pan of water to the boil. Break the eggs into separate cups, then carefully slide into the water. Gently poach the eggs for about 4 minutes until they are lightly cooked.

4 Meanwhile, divide the salad leaves between two plates. Remove the croûtons from the pan and arrange over the leaves. Wipe the frying pan clean with kitchen paper.

5 Heat the remaining oil in the frying pan and cook the garlic and vinegar over high heat for about 1 minute. Pour the warm dressing over the salad leaves and croûtons. Place a poached egg on each salad. Scatter with shavings of Parmesan cheese and a little freshly ground black pepper.

Cook's Tip
Add a dash of vinegar to the water before poaching the eggs. This helps to keep the whites together. To ensure that a poached egg has a good shape, swirl the water with a spoon before sliding in the egg.

Caesar Salad

A popular combination of crisp lettuce, crunchy croûtons and Parmesan cheese in a tasty egg dressing.

Serves 4

1 large cos or romaine lettuce
4 thick slices white or granary
    bread, without crusts
45ml/3 tbsp olive oil
1 garlic clove, crushed
75ml/5 tbsp freshly grated
    Parmesan cheese

For the dressing
1 egg
1 garlic clove, chopped
30ml/2 tbsp lemon juice
dash of Worcestershire sauce
3 anchovy fillets, chopped
120ml/4fl oz/½ cup olive oil
salt and ground black pepper

1 Preheat the oven to 220°C/425°F/Gas 7. Separate, rinse and dry the lettuce leaves. Tear the outer leaves roughly and chop the heart. Arrange the lettuce in a large salad bowl.

2 Dice the bread and mix with the olive oil and garlic in a separate bowl until the bread has soaked up the oil. Lay the bread dice on a baking sheet and place in the oven for about 6–8 minutes until golden. Remove and leave to cool.

3 To make the dressing, break the egg into the bowl of a food processor or blender and add the garlic, lemon juice, Worcestershire sauce and one of the anchovy fillets. Process until smooth.

4 With the motor running, pour in the olive oil in a thin stream until the dressing has the consistency of thin cream. Season to taste with salt and pepper, if needed.

5 Pour the dressing over the salad leaves and toss well, then toss in the garlic croûtons, Parmesan cheese and finally the remaining anchovies and serve immediately.

Cook's Tip
Keep an eye on the croûtons in the oven; don't let them burn.

Poached Egg Energy 632kcal/2641kJ; Protein 21g; Carbohydrate 50.3g, of which sugars 3.6g; Fat 40.1g, of which saturates 8.6g; Cholesterol 205mg; Calcium 335mg; Fibre 2g; Sodium 755mg.
Caesar Energy 420kcal/1740kJ; Protein 12.2g; Carbohydrate 13.6g, of which sugars 1.9g; Fat 35.6g, of which saturates 8.2g; Cholesterol 68mg; Calcium 288mg; Fibre 1.1g; Sodium 443mg.

Tuna & Bean Salad

This popular salad makes a good light meal, and can be very quickly assembled from store-cupboard ingredients.

Serves 4–6
2 x 400g/14oz cans cannellini or
  borlotti beans
2 x 200g/7oz cans tuna fish,
  drained

60ml/4 tbsp extra virgin olive oil
30ml/2 tbsp lemon juice
15ml/1 tbsp chopped fresh
  parsley
3 spring onions (scallions), thinly
  sliced
salt and ground black pepper
fresh parsley sprigs, to garnish
  (optional)

1 Pour the beans into a large sieve (strainer) and rinse under cold running water. Drain well. Place in a serving dish.

2 Break the tuna into fairly large flakes with a fork and arrange over the beans.

3 Make the dressing by combining the oil with the lemon juice in a small bowl. Season with salt and pepper, and stir in the parsley. Mix well. Pour the dressing over the beans and tuna.

4 Sprinkle the sliced spring onions over the salad and toss well. Garnish with parsley, if using, and serve immediately.

Cook's Tip
If you prefer a milder onion flavour, gently sauté the spring onions in a little oil until softened, before adding to the salad.

Variation
For a vegetarian version, roast, peel and dice 2 red (bell) peppers, saving any juices. Fry 1 large crushed garlic clove in 30ml/2 tbsp olive oil until soft, then add a handful of chopped parsley, the pepper and juices, plus 15ml/1 tbsp balsamic vinegar. Pour over the beans, toss together, season and serve.

Grilled Pepper Salad

This tangy salad hails from southern Italy where all the ingredients thrive in the Mediterranean sun. Serve as a colourful side salad for a cold spread, or as a fresh-tasting starter, topped with a sprinkling of basil.

Serves 6
4 large (bell) peppers, red or
  yellow or a combination of both

30ml/2 tbsp capers in salt,
  vinegar or brine, rinsed
18–20 black or green olives

For the dressing
90ml/6 tbsp extra virgin olive oil
2 garlic cloves, chopped
30ml/2 tbsp balsamic or wine
  vinegar
salt and ground black pepper

1 Place the whole peppers under a hot grill (broiler) and grill (broil), turning occasionally, until they are beginning to char and blister on all sides.

2 Put the charred peppers in a bowl, cover with kitchen paper and leave to cool for 10 minutes, then peel off the skins. Remove the seeds and cores, then cut the flesh into quarters.

3 Cut the peppers into strips and arrange them in a serving dish. Distribute the capers and olives evenly over them.

4 To make the dressing, mix the oil and garlic together in a small bowl, crushing the garlic with a spoon to release as much flavour as possible. Mix in the vinegar and season to taste with salt and pepper.

5 Pour the dressing over the salad, mix well and allow to stand for at least 30 minutes before serving.

Cook's Tip
Charring the peppers under the grill helps to bring out their delicious sweet flavour. It also lifts the skin from the pepper flesh, making peeling easy.

Bean Salad Energy 294kcal/1235kJ; Protein 27.4g; Carbohydrate 23.9g, of which sugars 4.9g; Fat 10.5g, of which saturates 1.7g; Cholesterol 33mg; Calcium 105mg; Fibre 8.4g; Sodium 714mg.
Pepper Salad Energy 148kcal/612kJ; Protein 1.5g; Carbohydrate 8g, of which sugars 7.2g; Fat 12.4g, of which saturates 1.8g; Cholesterol 0mg; Calcium 15mg; Fibre 2.3g; Sodium 192mg.

Warm Chicken Liver & Tomato Salad

Warm salads are especially welcome during the autumn months when the evenings are growing shorter and cooler. Serve with French bread for mopping up the delicious juices.

Serves 4

225g/8oz/4 cups young spinach, stems removed
1 frisée lettuce
105ml/7 tbsp groundnut (peanut) or sunflower oil
175g/6oz rindless bacon, cut into strips
3 slices day-old bread, without crusts, cut into short fingers
450g/1lb chicken livers
115g/4oz cherry tomatoes
salt and ground black pepper

1 Wash the spinach and the frisée lettuce leaves, then dry thoroughly in a salad spinner. Place in a salad bowl.

2 Heat 60ml/4 tbsp of the oil in a large frying pan and cook the bacon for 3–4 minutes until crisp and brown. Remove the bacon with a slotted spoon and leave to drain on a piece of kitchen paper.

3 To make the croûtons, fry the bread in the bacon-flavoured oil, tossing until crisp and golden. Drain on kitchen paper.

4 Heat the remaining 45ml/3 tbsp of oil in the frying pan and fry the chicken livers briskly for 2–3 minutes. Transfer the livers and pan juices to the salad leaves in the bowl, add the fried bacon, croûtons and cherry tomatoes. Season with salt and pepper, toss gently and serve.

Cook's Tip
Although fresh chicken livers are preferable, frozen ones could be used in this salad. It is important to make sure they are completely thawed before cooking.

Maryland Salad

A harmonious blend of sweet and savoury flavours, this salad makes a stunning main-course salad.

Serves 4

4 free-range chicken breast fillets
olive oil, for brushing
225g/8oz rindless unsmoked bacon
4 corn on the cob
40g/1½oz/3 tbsp butter, softened
4 ripe bananas, peeled and halved
4 firm tomatoes, halved
4 escarole or round (butterhead) lettuces
1 bunch watercress, weighing about 115g/4oz
salt and ground black pepper

For the dressing
75ml/5 tbsp groundnut (peanut) oil
15ml/1 tbsp white wine vinegar
5ml/1 tsp maple syrup
10ml/2 tsp mild mustard

1 Season the chicken fillets with salt and pepper, brush with oil and barbecue or grill (broil) for 15 minutes, turning once, until cooked through. Keep warm.

2 Barbecue or grill the bacon for 8–10 minutes or until crisp. Keep warm.

3 Bring a large pan of salted water to the boil. Trim and husk the corn on the cob, then add to the boiling water and cook for 20 minutes. Brush with butter and brown over the barbecue or under the grill.

4 Barbecue or grill the bananas and tomatoes for 6–8 minutes, brushing with butter, if you wish.

5 To make the dressing, combine the oil, vinegar, maple syrup and mustard with 15ml/1 tbsp water in a screw-top jar and shake well. Put the lettuce leaves in a bowl with the watercress, then toss with the dressing.

6 Divide the salad leaves among four large plates. Slice the chicken and arrange over the leaves with the bacon, banana, corn and tomatoes. Serve immediately.

Chicken Liver Energy 441kcal/1834kJ; Protein 31g; Carbohydrate 11.7g, of which sugars 3.5g; Fat 30.3g, of which saturates 6g; Cholesterol 451mg; Calcium 149mg; Fibre 2.4g; Sodium 934mg.
Maryland Energy 613kcal/2562kJ; Protein 48.9g; Carbohydrate 29.3g, of which sugars 26.8g; Fat 34.1g, of which saturates 12.2g; Cholesterol 156mg; Calcium 102mg; Fibre 3.3g; Sodium 1193mg.

Chicory, Fruit & Nut Salad

Mildly bitter chicory is wonderful with sweet fruit, and is delicious when complemented by a creamy curry sauce.

Serves 4
45ml/3 tbsp mayonnaise
15ml/1 tbsp Greek-style (US strained, plain) yogurt
15ml/1 tbsp mild curry paste
90ml/6 tbsp single (light) cream
½ iceberg lettuce
2 heads chicory (Belgian endive)
50g/2oz/1 cup flaked coconut
50g/2oz/½ cup cashew nuts
2 red eating apples
75g/3oz/½ cup currants

1 Mix together the mayonnaise, Greek-style yogurt, curry paste and single cream in a small bowl. Cover and chill until required.

2 Tear the iceberg lettuce into even-size pieces and put into a salad bowl.

3 Cut the root end off each head of chicory and discard. Slice the chicory, or separate the leaves, and add to the salad bowl. Preheat the grill (broiler).

4 Spread out the coconut flakes on a baking sheet. Grill (broil) for 1 minute until golden. Turn into a bowl and set aside. Toast the cashew nuts for 2 minutes until golden.

5 Quarter the apples and cut out the cores. Slice the apple quarters and add to the lettuce with the toasted coconut, cashew nuts and currants.

6 Stir up the chilled dressing and pour over the salad. Toss lightly together and serve immediately.

> **Cook's Tip**
> Choose a sweet, well-flavoured variety of red apple for this salad, such as Royal Gala. Leave on the skins to provide added colour and texture.

Spicy Sweetcorn Salad

This brilliant, sweet-flavoured salad is served warm with a delicious, spicy dressing.

Serves 4
30ml/2 tbsp vegetable oil
450g/1lb drained canned sweetcorn, or frozen sweetcorn, thawed
1 green (bell) pepper, seeded and diced
1 small red chilli, seeded and finely diced
4 spring onions (scallions), sliced
45ml/3 tbsp chopped fresh parsley
225g/8oz cherry tomatoes, halved
salt and ground black pepper

For the dressing
2.5ml/½ tsp sugar
30ml/2 tbsp white wine vinegar
2.5ml/½ tsp Dijon mustard
15ml/1 tbsp chopped fresh basil
15ml/1 tbsp mayonnaise
1.5ml/¼ tsp chilli sauce

1 Heat the oil in a frying pan. Add the sweetcorn, green pepper, chilli and spring onions. Cook over medium heat for about 5 minutes, until softened, stirring frequently.

2 Transfer the vegetables to a salad bowl. Stir in the parsley and the cherry tomatoes.

3 To make the dressing, combine all the ingredients in a small bowl and whisk together.

4 Pour the dressing over the sweetcorn mixture. Season with salt and pepper to taste. Toss well to combine, then serve immediately, while the salad is still warm.

> **Cook's Tip**
> Don't touch your eyes with your hands while preparing the chilli.

> **Variation**
> If serving the salad to children, you can make the flavour milder by omitting the fresh chilli and the chilli sauce.

Chicory Energy 323kcal/1347kJ; Protein 5.7g; Carbohydrate 22.5g, of which sugars 19.8g; Fat 24.1g, of which saturates 8.7g; Cholesterol 21mg; Calcium 105mg; Fibre 4g; Sodium 122mg.
Sweetcorn Energy 245kcal/1032kJ; Protein 4.7g; Carbohydrate 35.9g, of which sugars 16.6g; Fat 10.2g, of which saturates 1.4g; Cholesterol 3mg; Calcium 39mg; Fibre 3.6g; Sodium 338mg.

Tomato & Bread Salad

This salad is a traditional peasant dish from Tuscany and was created to use up bread that was several days old. The success of the dish depends on the quality of the tomatoes – they must be ripe and well flavoured. Serve with a green salad for a good contrast in colour and texture.

Serves 4

400g/14oz stale white or brown
    bread or rolls

4 large tomatoes

1 large red onion, or 6 spring
    onions (scallions)

a few fresh basil leaves, to garnish

For the dressing

60ml/4 tbsp extra virgin olive oil

30ml/2 tbsp white wine vinegar

salt and ground black pepper

1 Cut the bread or rolls into thick slices. Place in a shallow bowl and add enough cold water to soak the bread. Leave for at least 30 minutes.

2 Cut the tomatoes into chunks and place in a serving bowl. Finely slice the onion or spring onions and add them to the tomatoes. Squeeze as much water out of the bread as possible. Add the bread to the vegetables.

3 To make the dressing, whisk the olive oil with the vinegar, then season with salt and pepper.

4 Pour the dressing over the salad and mix well. Decorate with the basil leaves. Allow to stand in a cool place for a least 2 hours before serving.

> **Cook's Tip**
> *Tomatoes left to ripen on the vine will have the best flavour so try to buy "vine-ripened" varieties. If you can only find unripened tomatoes, you can help them along by putting them in a paper bag with a ripe tomato or leaving them in a fruit bowl with a banana; the gases the ripe fruits give off will ripen them, but, unfortunately, this process cannot improve the flavour.*

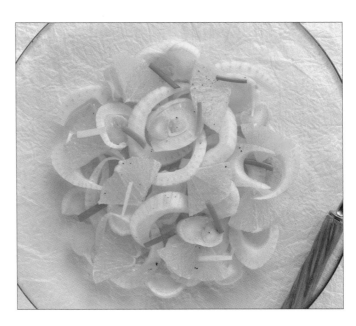

Fennel & Orange Salad

This light and refreshing salad originated in Sicily, following the old custom of serving fennel at the end of a meal, to help digestion. The delicate aniseed flavour of the fennel marries well with sweet oranges.

Serves 4

2 large fennel bulbs (about
    675g/1½ lb total)

2 sweet oranges

2 spring onions (scallions),
    to garnish

For the dressing

60ml/4 tbsp extra virgin olive oil

30ml/2 tbsp fresh lemon juice

salt and ground black pepper

1 Wash the fennel bulbs and remove any brown or stringy outer leaves. Slice the bulbs and stems into thin pieces. Place in a shallow serving bowl.

2 Peel the oranges with a sharp knife, cutting away the white pith. Slice thinly. Cut each slice into thirds. Arrange over the fennel, adding any juice from the oranges.

3 To make the dressing, mix the oil and lemon juice together. Season with salt and pepper. Pour the dressing over the salad and mix well.

4 Slice the white and green sections of the spring onions thinly. Sprinkle over the salad and serve immediately.

> **Cook's Tips**
> • *For a delicate orange rind garnish to enhance the flavour of the salad, use a vegetable peeler to cut thin strips of rind from the unpeeled oranges, leaving the pith behind. Then cut the pieces into thin matchstick strips and cook in a small pan of boiling water for 2–3 minutes. Drain and dry on kitchen paper, then sprinkle on top of the salad before serving.*
> • *When buying fennel, choose firm round bulbs. The outer layers should be crisp and white, with the texture of green celery.*

Tomato Energy 369kcal/1557kJ; Protein 9.7g; Carbohydrate 56.4g, of which sugars 8.5g; Fat 13.3g, of which saturates 1.7g; Cholesterol 0mg; Calcium 130mg; Fibre 3.2g; Sodium 531mg.
Fennel Energy 148kcal/614kJ; Protein 2.5g; Carbohydrate 9.6g, of which sugars 9.4g; Fat 11.4g, of which saturates 1.6g; Cholesterol 0mg; Calcium 78mg; Fibre 5.4g; Sodium 23mg.

Haddock with Parsley Sauce

The parsley sauce is enriched with cream and an egg yolk in this simple supper dish.

Serves 4
4 haddock fillets (about 175g/
   6oz each)
50g/2oz/4 tbsp butter
150ml/¼ pint/⅔ cup milk
150ml/¼ pint/⅔ cup fish stock

1 bay leaf
20ml/4 tsp plain (all-
   purpose) flour
60ml/4 tbsp double
   (heavy) cream
1 egg yolk
45ml/3 tbsp chopped
   fresh parsley
grated rind and juice of ½ lemon
salt and ground black pepper

1 Place the fish in a frying pan, add half the butter, the milk, fish stock and bay leaf and season with salt and pepper. Bring to simmering point over medium-low heat. Lower the heat, cover the pan with a tight-fitting lid and poach the fish for 10–15 minutes, depending on the thickness of the fillets, until the fish is tender and the flesh just begins to flake.

2 Transfer the fish to a warmed serving plate with a slotted spoon, cover it and keep warm while you make the sauce.

3 Return the cooking liquid to the heat and bring to the boil, stirring constantly. Simmer for about 4 minutes, then remove and discard the bay leaf.

4 Melt the remaining butter in a pan, add the flour and cook, stirring constantly, for 1 minute. Remove from the heat and gradually stir in the fish cooking liquid. Return to the heat and bring to the boil, stirring constantly. Simmer for about 4 minutes, stirring frequently.

5 Remove the pan from the heat, blend the cream into the egg yolk, then stir into the sauce with the parsley. Reheat gently, stirring for a few minutes, but do not let it to boil. Remove from the heat, add the lemon juice and rind and season to taste with salt and pepper. Pour the sauce into a warmed sauceboat and serve immediately with the fish.

Pickled Herrings

A good basic pickled herring dish which is enhanced by the grainy mustard vinaigrette.

Serves 4
4 fresh herrings, gutted
   and boned
150ml/¼ pint/⅔ cup white
   wine vinegar
2 tsp salt

12 black peppercorns
2 bay leaves
4 cloves
2 small onions, sliced

For the dressing
1 tsp coarse grain mustard
3 tbsp olive oil
1 tbsp white wine vinegar
salt and ground black pepper

1 Preheat the oven to 160C°/325°F/Gas 3. Cut each fish into two fillets with a sharp knife.

2 Roll up the fillets tightly and place them in an ovenproof dish, closely packed together so that they can't unroll.

3 Pour the vinegar over the fish and add just enough water to cover them.

4 Add the salt, peppercorns, bay leaves, cloves and onions, cover and bake for 1 hour. Remove the fish from the oven and leave to cool in the liquid.

5 To make the dressing, put all the ingredients in a screw-top jar, close the lid and shake well to combine. Serve the fish with the dressing poured over the top.

Variation
Cook soused herrings in the same way, substituting malt vinegar for the wine vinegar, 5ml/1 tsp allspice for the peppercorns and 5ml/1 tsp pickling spice for the cloves and adding 5ml/1 tsp sugar to the mixture. Soused herrings are usually served cold – with or without the dressing from the recipe above – but may also be served hot with boiled potatoes.

Haddock Energy 317kcal/1332kJ; Protein 35.9g; Carbohydrate 8.5g, of which sugars 0.9g; Fat 15.9g, of which saturates 8.9g; Cholesterol 148mg; Calcium 85mg; Fibre 0.9g; Sodium 204mg.
Herrings Energy 231kcal/963kJ; Protein 12.5g; Carbohydrate 7.5g, of which sugars 7.5g; Fat 16.6g, of which saturates 1.2g; Cholesterol 32mg; Calcium 10mg; Fibre 0g; Sodium 623mg.

Herrings in Oatmeal with Mustard

In this delicious dish, crunchy-coated herrings are served with a piquant mustard sauce.

Serves 4

about 15ml/1 tbsp Dijon mustard
about 7.5ml/1½ tsp tarragon
   vinegar
175ml/6fl oz/¾ cup thick
   mayonnaise
4 herrings (about 225g/8oz
   each), gutted
1 lemon, halved
115g/4oz/1 cup medium oatmeal
salt and ground black pepper

1 Beat the mustard and vinegar to taste into the mayonnaise. Chill lightly in the refrigerator.

2 Place one fish at a time on a chopping board, cut-side down and opened out. Press gently all along the backbone with your thumbs. Turn the fish over and carefully lift away the backbone and discard.

3 Squeeze lemon juice over both sides of each fish, then season with salt and ground black pepper. Fold the fish in half, skin-side outwards.

4 Preheat the grill (broiler) until fairly hot. Place the oatmeal on a shallow plate, then coat each herring evenly in the oatmeal, pressing it on gently with your fingers.

5 Place the herrings on a grill (broiler) rack and grill (broil) the fish for about 3–4 minutes on each side, until the skin is golden brown and crisp and the flesh flakes easily. Serve hot with the mustard sauce, served separately.

Variation
For extra flavour coarsely chop 4 rashers (strips) of streaky (fatty) bacon and dry-fry in a heavy frying pan over low heat until golden and crisp. Drain on kitchen paper. Sprinkle the bacon over the cooked fish before serving.

Smoked Trout with Cucumber

Smoked trout provides an easy and delicious first course or light meal. Serve at room temperature for the best flavour.

Serves 4

1 large cucumber
60ml/4 tbsp crème fraîche
   or Greek (US strained
   plain) yogurt
15ml/1 tbsp chopped
   fresh dill
4 smoked trout fillets
salt and ground black pepper
fresh dill sprigs, to garnish
crusty wholemeal (whole-wheat)
   bread, to serve

1 Peel the cucumber, cut in half lengthways and scoop out the seeds using a teaspoon. Cut the flesh into tiny dice.

2 Put the cucumber in a colander set over a plate and sprinkle with salt. Leave to drain for at least 1 hour to draw out the excess moisture.

3 Rinse the cucumber well, then pat dry on kitchen paper. Transfer the diced cucumber to a bowl and stir in the crème fraîche or yogurt, chopped dill and some freshly ground pepper. Chill the cucumber salad for about 30 minutes.

4 Arrange the trout fillets on individual plates. Spoon the cucumber and dill salad on one side and grind over a little black pepper. Garnish the dish with dill sprigs and serve immediately with crusty bread.

Cook's Tip
Trout is hot-smoked at a temperature of 75–100°C/ 167–212°F, which, in effect, cooks it at the same time. It, therefore, needs no further cooking. If you are planning to substitute another fish, make sure that it has also been hot-smoked, as, with the exception of salmon, most cold-smoked fish requires further cooking.

Herrings Energy 721kcal/2997kJ; Protein 35.3g; Carbohydrate 21.7g, of which sugars 0.6g; Fat 55.4g, of which saturates 10.6g; Cholesterol 109mg; Calcium 69mg; Fibre 2g; Sodium 476mg.
Smoked trout Energy 146kcal/606kJ; Protein 15.2g; Carbohydrate 1.1g, of which sugars 1g; Fat 8.9g, of which saturates 4.1g; Cholesterol 17mg; Calcium 25mg; Fibre 0.3g; Sodium 47mg.

Crunchy-topped Cod

It's easy to forget just how tasty and satisfying a simple, classic dish can be.

Serves 4
4 pieces cod fillet (about 115g/4oz each), skinned
2 tomatoes, sliced

50g/2oz/1 cup fresh wholemeal (whole-wheat) breadcrumbs
30ml/2 tbsp chopped fresh parsley
finely grated rind and juice of ½ lemon
5ml/1 tsp sunflower oil
salt and ground black pepper

1 Preheat the oven to 200°C/400°F/Gas 6. Arrange the cod fillets in a wide, ovenproof dish.

2 Arrange the tomato slices on top. Mix together the breadcrumbs, fresh parsley, lemon rind and juice and the oil in a bowl. Season to taste with salt and pepper.

3 Spoon the crumb mixture evenly over the fish, then bake for 15–20 minutes. Serve immediately.

Cook's Tip

Over-fishing of cod – and some other members of the cod family – has reached a critical level in many parts of the world with the result that some stocks have been completely fished-out. Conservation initiatives are having some remedial effect, so it is strongly advised to check that the cod we are buying comes from a sustainable source. Otherwise, we may lose this useful fish with its lovely, white flaky flesh. Other members of the cod family that have not been so popular in recent decades are becoming increasingly available and some would make very acceptable substitutes in this dish. For example, coley, known as pollock in the United States, has a good flavour but is a rather unappealing greyish colour. However, the crunchy topping in this recipe overcomes this drawback. The various types of ling also have a good flavour and a firm texture and this is also true of another lesser known cousin of cod called pollack (not to be confused with pollock).

Mackerel with Tomatoes & Pesto

This rich and oily fish contrasts superbly with the slight sharpness of the tomato sauce. The aromatic pesto is excellent drizzled over the fish.

Serves 4
For the pesto sauce
50g/2oz/½ cup pine nuts
30ml/2 tbsp fresh basil leaves
2 garlic cloves, crushed

30ml/2 tbsp freshly grated Parmesan cheese
150ml/¼ pint/⅔ cup extra virgin olive oil

For the fish
4 fresh mackerel, gutted
30ml/2 tbsp olive oil
115g/4oz onion, coarsely chopped
450g/1lb tomatoes, coarsely chopped
salt and ground black pepper

1 To make the pesto sauce, place the pine nuts, basil and garlic cloves in a food processor fitted with a metal blade. Process until the mixture forms a coarse paste. Add the Parmesan cheese and, with the motor still running, gradually add the oil. Set aside in a cool place until required.

2 Preheat the grill (broiler) until very hot. Season the mackerel well with salt and pepper, place on the grill (broiler) rack and cook for 10 minutes on each side.

3 Meanwhile, heat the olive oil in a large, heavy pan over low heat. Add the onion and cook, stirring occasionally, for about 5 minutes, until softened but not coloured.

4 Stir in the tomatoes and cook, stirring occasionally, for 5–10 minutes, until just pulpy. Spoon the tomato mixture on to warmed serving plates, add the fish and top each one with a spoonful of pesto sauce. Serve immediately.

Cook's Tip

The pesto sauce can be made ahead and stored in the refrigerator until needed. Soften it again before using. For red pesto sauce, add some puréed sun-dried tomatoes after the oil.

Cod Energy 160kcal/674kJ; Protein 24.7g; Carbohydrate 11.3g, of which sugars 1.9g; Fat 2g, of which saturates 0.3g; Cholesterol 58mg; Calcium 31mg; Fibre 0.8g; Sodium 175mg.
Mackerel Energy 759kcal/3145kJ; Protein 39.3g; Carbohydrate 6.3g, of which sugars 5.6g; Fat 64.2g, of which saturates 11.6g; Cholesterol 100mg; Calcium 126mg; Fibre 1.8g; Sodium 194mg.

Mackerel with Mustard & Lemon

Mackerel must be really fresh to be enjoyed. Look for bright, firm-fleshed fish with iridescent scales and clear, unsunken eyes.

Serves 4
4 fresh mackerel (about 275g/10oz each), gutted
175–225g/6–8oz/1½–2 cups spinach
salt and ground black pepper

For the mustard and lemon butter
115g/4oz/½ cup butter, melted
30ml/2 tbsp wholegrain mustard
grated rind of 1 lemon
30ml/2 tbsp lemon juice
45ml/3 tbsp chopped fresh parsley

1 To prepare each mackerel, use a sharp knife to cut off the head just behind the gills, then cut along the belly so that the fish can be opened out flat.

2 Place the fish on a chopping board, skin-side up, and press firmly all along the backbone to loosen it.

3 Turn the fish over and carefully pull the bone away from the flesh. Remove the tail and cut each fish in half lengthways. Rinse under cold running water and pat dry with kitchen paper. Score the skin three or four times, then season the fish all over with salt and pepper. Preheat the grill (broiler).

4 To make the mustard and lemon butter, mix together the melted butter, mustard, lemon rind and juice and parsley. Season with salt and pepper.

5 Place the mackerel on a grill (broiler) rack. Brush a little of the flavoured butter over the mackerel and grill (broil), basting occasionally, for 5 minutes on each side, until cooked through.

6 Arrange the spinach leaves in the centres of four large plates. Place the mackerel on top. Heat the remaining mustard and lemon butter in a small pan until sizzling and pour it over the mackerel. Serve immediately.

Whitebait with Herb Sandwiches

Whitebait are the tiny fry of sprats or herring and are always served whole. Cayenne pepper makes them spicy hot.

Serves 4
unsalted (sweet) butter, for spreading
6 slices multigrain bread
90ml/6 tbsp mixed chopped fresh herbs, such as parsley, chervil and chives

450g/1lb whitebait, thawed if frozen
65g/2½ oz/scant ¾ cup plain (all-purpose) flour
15ml/1 tbsp chopped fresh parsley
salt and cayenne pepper
groundnut (peanut) oil, for deep-frying
lemon slices, to garnish

1 Butter the bread slices. Sprinkle the herbs over three of the slices, then top with the remaining slices of bread. Remove the crusts and cut each sandwich into eight triangles. Place them on a plate, cover with clear film (plastic wrap) and set aside in a cool place.

2 Rinse the whitebait thoroughly under cold running water. Drain and then pat dry on kitchen paper.

3 Put the flour, chopped parsley, salt and cayenne pepper in a large plastic bag and shake to mix. Add the whitebait, a few at a time, and toss gently in the seasoned flour, until lightly coated. Heat the oil in a deep-fat fryer or large, heavy pan to 180°C/350°F, or until a cube of day-old bread browns in 30 seconds.

4 Lower the fish into the hot oil, in batches, and cook for 2–3 minutes, until golden and crisp. Lift out of the oil and drain well on kitchen paper. Keep warm in the oven until all the fish are cooked.

5 Sprinkle the whitebait with salt and more cayenne pepper, if you like, and garnish with the lemon slices. Serve immediately with the herb sandwiches.

Mackerel Energy 723kcal/2995kJ; Protein 44.7g; Carbohydrate 1.2g, of which sugars 1.1g; Fat 59.9g, of which saturates 22.5g; Cholesterol 181mg; Calcium 124mg; Fibre 1.4g; Sodium 369mg.
Whitebait Energy 776kcal/3222kJ; Protein 26.7g; Carbohydrate 27.7g, of which sugars 1.8g; Fat 62.9g, of which saturates 10.4g; Cholesterol 21mg; Calcium 1088mg; Fibre 2.3g; Sodium 569mg.

Trout with Hazelnuts

The hazelnuts in this recipe make an interesting change from the almonds that are more often used.

Serves 4

50g/2oz/½ cup hazelnuts, chopped

65g/2½oz/5 tbsp butter
4 trout (about 275g/10oz each), gutted
30ml/2 tbsp lemon juice
salt and ground black pepper
lemon slices and fresh flat leaf parsley sprigs, to serve

1 Preheat the grill (broiler). Toast the nuts in a single layer, stirring frequently, until the skins split. Then transfer the nuts to a clean dish towel and rub to remove the skins. Leave the nuts to cool, then chop them coarsely.

2 Heat 50g/2oz/4 tbsp of the butter in a large frying pan. Season the trout inside and out with salt and pepper, then cook them, two at a time, for 12–15 minutes, turning once, until the trout are brown and the flesh flakes easily when tested with the point of a sharp kitchen knife.

3 Drain the cooked trout on kitchen paper, then transfer to a warm serving plate and keep warm while frying the remaining trout in the same way. (If your frying pan is large enough, you could, of course, cook the trout in one batch.)

4 Add the remaining butter to the frying pan and fry the hazelnuts until evenly browned. Stir the lemon juice into the pan and mix well, then quickly pour the buttery sauce over the trout and serve immediately, garnished with slices of lemon and flat leaf parsley sprigs.

Cook's Tip
You can use a microwave to prepare the nuts instead of the grill (broiler). Spread them out in a shallow microwave dish and leave uncovered. Cook on full power until the skins split, then remove the skins using a dish towel as described above.

Trout Wrapped in a Blanket

The "blanket" of bacon bastes the fish during cooking, keeping it moist and adding flavour at the same time.

Serves 4

butter, for greasing
juice of ½ lemon
4 trout (about 275g/10oz each), gutted

4 fresh thyme sprigs, plus extra to garnish
8 thin rashers (strips) rindless streaky (fatty) bacon
salt and ground black pepper
chopped fresh parsley, to garnish
lemon wedges, to serve

1 Preheat the oven to 200°C/400°F/Gas 6. Lightly grease a shallow ovenproof dish with butter.

2 Squeeze lemon juice over the skin and inside the cavity of each fish, season all over with salt and ground black pepper, then put a thyme sprig in each cavity.

3 Stretch each bacon rasher using the back of a knife, then wrap two rashers around each fish. Place the fish in the prepared dish, with the loose ends of bacon tucked underneath to prevent them from unwinding.

4 Bake the trout for 15–20 minutes, until the flesh flakes easily when tested with the point of a sharp knife and the bacon is crisp and beginning to brown.

5 Transfer the fish to warmed individual plates and serve immediately garnished with chopped parsley and sprigs of thyme and accompanied by lemon wedges.

Variation
Smoked streaky (fatty) bacon will impart a stronger flavour to the fish. If you like, use chopped fresh coriander (cilantro) in place of the parsley for the garnish.

With Hazelnuts Energy 414kcal/1723kJ; Protein 38.7g; Carbohydrate 0.9g, of which sugars 0.6g; Fat 28.4g, of which saturates 10.7g; Cholesterol 187mg; Calcium 78mg; Fibre 0.8g; Sodium 237mg.
In a blanket Energy 316kcal/1323kJ; Protein 42.8g; Carbohydrate 0.1g, of which sugars 0.1g; Fat 16g, of which saturates 4.8g; Cholesterol 176mg; Calcium 64mg; Fibre 0.1g; Sodium 611mg.

Smoked Trout Pilaff

Smoked trout might seem a rather unusual partner for rice, but if you try it, you will find that this is a winning combination.

Serves 4
225g/8oz/1¼ cups white
   basmati rice
40g/1½oz/3 tbsp butter
2 onions, sliced into rings
1 garlic clove, crushed
2 bay leaves
2 whole cloves
2 green cardamom pods
2 cinnamon sticks
5ml/1 tsp cumin seeds
4 smoked trout fillets, skinned
50g/2oz/½ cup slivered
   almonds, toasted
50g/2oz/generous ½ cup
   seedless raisins
30ml/2 tbsp chopped
   fresh parsley or
   coriander (cilantro)
mango chutney and poppadoms,
   to serve

1 Wash the rice thoroughly in several changes of water and, if there is time, leave to soak in cold water for 10–15 minutes. Drain well and set aside.

2 Melt the butter in a large pan over low heat. Add the onions and cook, stirring occasionally, for 10–20 minutes, until well browned.

3 Increase the heat, add the garlic, bay leaves, cloves, cardamom pods, cinnamon and cumin seeds and stir-fry for 1 minute.

4 Stir in the rice, then add 600ml/1 pint/2½ cups boiling water. Bring back to the boil, cover the pan with a tight-fitting lid, lower the heat and cook very gently for 20–25 minutes, until the water has been absorbed and the rice is tender.

5 Flake the smoked trout and add to the pan with the almonds and raisins. Fork through gently, then re-cover the pan and leave the smoked trout to warm in the rice for a few minutes.

6 Transfer the pilaff to warmed plates, sprinkle the parsley or coriander over the top and serve immediately with mango chutney and poppadoms.

Fish Balls in Tomato Sauce

This quick meal is a good choice for young children, as there are no bones.

Serves 4
450g/1lb hoki or other white fish
   fillets, skinned
60ml/4 tbsp fresh wholemeal
   (whole-wheat) breadcrumbs
30ml/2 tbsp chopped chives or
   spring onion (scallion)
400g/14oz can chopped
   tomatoes
50g/2oz button (white)
   mushrooms, sliced
salt and ground black pepper

1 Cut the fish fillets into chunks; place in a food processor. Add the breadcrumbs, chives or spring onion. Season and process until the fish is chopped, but still with some texture. Divide the fish mixture into about 16 even-sized pieces, then mould them into balls with your hands.

2 Place the tomatoes and mushrooms in a pan; cook over medium heat until boiling. Add the fish balls, cover and simmer for about 10 minutes until cooked. Serve hot.

Tuna & Corn Fish Cakes

These economical tuna fish cakes are quick to make.

Serves 4
300g/11oz/1½ cups mashed
   potato
200g/7oz can tuna, drained
115g/4oz/½ cup canned
   corn, drained
30ml/2 tbsp chopped
   fresh parsley
50g/2oz/1 cup fresh
   breadcrumbs
salt and ground black pepper

1 Place the mashed potato in a bowl and stir in the tuna, corn and parsley. Season to taste and shape into eight patties.

2 Press the fish cakes into the breadcrumbs to coat them lightly, then place on a baking sheet. Grill (broil) under medium heat until crisp and golden, turning once. Serve immediately.

Trout Energy 536kcal/2238kJ; Protein 27.8g; Carbohydrate 62.5g, of which sugars 14.9g; Fat 19.6g, of which saturates 5.8g; Cholesterol 21mg; Calcium 90mg; Fibre 2.8g; Sodium 130mg.
Fish Balls Energy 167kcal/709kJ; Protein 21.7g; Carbohydrate 14.8g, of which sugars 3.5g; Fat 2.8g, of which saturates 0.5g; Cholesterol 0mg; Calcium 44mg; Fibre 1.5g; Sodium 221mg.
Fish Cakes Energy 231kcal/976kJ; Protein 17.5g; Carbohydrate 29.8g, of which sugars 4.4g; Fat 5.5g, of which saturates 0.9g; Cholesterol 25mg; Calcium 53mg; Fibre 2.1g; Sodium 330mg.

Warm Salmon Salad

This light salad is perfect in summer. Serve it as soon as it is ready, or the salad leaves will lose their colour.

Serves 4
450g/1lb salmon fillet
30ml/2 tbsp sesame oil
grated rind of ½ orange
juice of 1 orange
5ml/1 tsp Dijon mustard
15ml/1 tbsp chopped
   fresh tarragon

45ml/3 tbsp groundnut
   (peanut) oil
115g/4oz fine green beans,
   trimmed
175g/6oz mixed salad leaves,
   such as young spinach leaves,
   radicchio and frisée
15ml/1 tbsp toasted sesame
   seeds
salt and ground black pepper

1 Skin the salmon fillet, if this has not already been done by your fish supplier, and cut the flesh into bitesize pieces with a sharp knife. Set aside.

2 To make the dressing, mix together the sesame oil, orange rind and juice, mustard and chopped tarragon in a bowl and season to taste with salt and ground black pepper. Set aside.

3 Heat the groundnut oil in a heavy frying pan over medium heat. Add the pieces of salmon and cook, stirring occasionally, for 3–4 minutes, or until lightly browned on the outside but still tender on the inside.

4 While the salmon is cooking, blanch the green beans in a pan of boiling salted water for 5–6 minutes, until tender but still slightly crisp.

5 Add the dressing to the salmon, toss together gently and cook for 30 seconds. Remove the pan from the heat.

6 Arrange the salad leaves on serving plates. Drain the beans and toss them over the leaves. Spoon the salmon and its cooking juices over the top, sprinkle with the toasted sesame seeds and serve immediately.

Red Mullet with Fennel

The delicately flavoured, almost sweet flesh of the fish is beautifully complemented by the aniseed-like taste of fennel.

Serves 4
3 small fennel bulbs
60ml/4 tbsp olive oil

2 small onions, sliced
2–4 fresh basil leaves
4 small or 2 large red mullet or
   snapper, gutted
grated rind of ½ lemon
150ml/¼ pint/⅔ cup fish stock
50g/2oz/4 tbsp butter
juice of 1 lemon

1 Snip off the feathery fronds from the fennel bulbs, finely chop and reserve them for the garnish. Cut the fennel bulb into wedges, being careful to leave the layers attached at the root ends so that the pieces stay intact.

2 Heat the oil in a frying pan large enough to take the fish in a single layer. Add the wedges of fennel and the onions and cook over low heat, stirring occasionally, for 10–15 minutes, until softened and lightly browned.

3 Tuck a basil leaf inside the cavity of each fish, then place them on top of the vegetables. Sprinkle the lemon rind on top. Increase the heat to medium, pour in the stock and bring just to the boil. Lower the heat, cover with a tight-fitting lid and poach gently for 15–20 minutes, until the fish is tender.

4 Melt the butter in a small pan and, when it starts to sizzle and colour slightly, add the lemon juice. Pour the flavoured butter over the fish, sprinkle with the reserved fennel fronds and serve immediately.

Cook's Tip
Other fish with fine-flavoured flesh may also be cooked this way. These include sea bass, sea bream, porgy and goatfish. It's best to trim the fins of all types and it is essential with those that have sharp spines.

Salmon Energy 362kcal/1499kJ; Protein 24.3g; Carbohydrate 1.7g, of which sugars 1.4g; Fat 28.7g, of which saturates 5g; Cholesterol 56mg; Calcium 72mg; Fibre 1.3g; Sodium 53mg.
Red Mullet Energy 330kcal/1369kJ; Protein 20.7g; Carbohydrate 4.3g, of which sugars 3.6g; Fat 25.8g, of which saturates 8.1g; Cholesterol 27mg; Calcium 111mg; Fibre 3.4g; Sodium 190mg.

Tuna with Pan-fried Tomatoes

Meaty and filling tuna steaks are served here with juicy tomatoes and black olives.

Serves 2

2 tuna steaks (about 175g/
  6oz each)
90ml/6 tbsp olive oil
30ml/2 tbsp lemon juice
2 garlic cloves, chopped

5ml/1 tsp chopped fresh thyme
4 canned anchovy fillets, drained
  and chopped
225g/8oz plum tomatoes, halved
30ml/2 tbsp chopped
  fresh parsley
4–6 black olives, pitted
  and chopped
pinch of ground black pepper
crusty bread, to serve

1 Place the tuna steaks in a shallow, non-metallic dish. Mix 60ml/4 tbsp of the oil with the lemon juice, garlic, thyme, anchovies and black pepper in a jug (pitcher). Pour this mixture over the tuna, cover and leave to marinate for at least 1 hour.

2 Preheat the grill (broiler). Lift the tuna from the marinade and place on a grill (broiler) rack. Grill (broil) for 4 minutes on each side, or until the tuna feels firm to touch, basting with the marinade. Take care not to overcook.

3 Meanwhile, heat the remaining oil in a frying pan and cook the tomatoes for a maximum of 2 minutes on each side.

4 Divide the tomatoes equally between two serving plates and sprinkle the chopped parsley and olives over them. Top each with a tuna steak.

5 Add the remaining marinade to the pan juices and warm through. Pour over the tomatoes and tuna steaks and serve immediately with crusty bread for mopping up the juices.

Cook's Tip
If you are unable to find fresh tuna steaks, you could replace them with salmon fillets, if you like – just grill (broil) them for one or two minutes more on each side.

Sautéed Salmon with Cucumber

Cucumber is the classic accompaniment to salmon. Here it is served hot, but be careful not to overcook it.

Serves 4
450g/1lb salmon fillet
40g/1½oz/3 tbsp butter
2 spring onions
  (scallions), chopped

½ cucumber, seeded and cut
  into strips
60ml/4 tbsp dry white wine
120ml/4fl oz/½ cup crème
  fraîche
30ml/2 tbsp chopped fresh chives
2 tomatoes, peeled, seeded and
  diced
salt and ground black pepper

1 Skin the salmon fillet, if this has not already been done by your fish supplier. Using a very sharp knife cut the flesh into about 12 thin slices, then cut across into strips.

2 Melt the butter in a large frying pan over medium-low heat. Add the salmon and cook, stirring occasionally, for 1–2 minutes. Remove the salmon strips using a slotted spoon and set aside.

3 Add the spring onions to the pan and cook for 2 minutes. Stir in the cucumber and sauté for 1–2 minutes, until hot. Remove the cucumber and keep warm with the salmon.

4 Add the wine to the pan and let it bubble until well reduced. Stir in the cucumber, crème fraîche and half the chives and season to taste with salt and pepper. Return the salmon to the pan and warm through gently. Sprinkle the tomatoes and remaining chives over the top. Serve immediately.

Cook's Tip
To skin a fish fillet, place it on a chopping board with the tail end towards you. Hold a sharp knife at an angle down towards the skin. Cut between the skin and the flesh, keeping the blade as close to the skin as possible. As the flesh is cut away, grasp the skin firmly with your other hand and continue cutting. A little salt sprinkled on your fingers makes this task less slippery.

Tuna Energy 757kcal/3135kJ; Protein 32.8g; Carbohydrate 4.8g, of which sugars 4.5g; Fat 67.7g, of which saturates 18.8g; Cholesterol 130mg; Calcium 93mg; Fibre 2.4g; Sodium 1138mg.
Salmon Energy 412kcal/1709kJ; Protein 24.1g; Carbohydrate 3g, of which sugars 2.8g; Fat 32.8g, of which saturates 15.5g; Cholesterol 111mg; Calcium 54mg; Fibre 0.7g; Sodium 124mg.

Fish Goujons

Any white fish fillets can be used to make these goujons – you could try a mixture of haddock and cod.

Serves 4
60ml/4 tbsp mayonnaise
30ml/2 tbsp natural (plain) yogurt
grated rind of ½ lime
squeeze of lime juice
15ml/1 tbsp chopped
   fresh parsley
15ml/1 tbsp capers, drained
   and chopped

2 sole fillets (about 175g/6oz
   each)
2 plaice or flounder fillets (about
   175g/6oz each)
1 egg
115g/4oz/2 cups fresh
   white breadcrumbs
15ml/1 tbsp sesame seeds
pinch of paprika
vegetable oil, for deep-frying
salt and ground black pepper
watercress or mizuna, to garnish
4 lime wedges, to serve

1 To make the lemon mayonnaise, mix the mayonnaise, yogurt, lime rind and juice, parsley and capers in a bowl. Cover with clear film (plastic wrap) and chill until required.

2 Skin the fish fillets if this has not already been done by your fish supplier and cut them into thin strips with a sharp knife.

3 Lightly beat the egg in a shallow bowl with a fork. Mix together the breadcrumbs, sesame seeds and paprika in another shallow bowl and season with salt and pepper.

4 Dip the fish strips, one at a time, first into the beaten egg, then into the breadcrumb mixture and toss until coated evenly. Lay on a clean plate.

5 Heat about 2.5cm/1in of vegetable oil in a frying pan to 180°C/350°F, or until a cube of day-old bread browns in 30 seconds. Add the fish strips, in batches, and cook for 2–3 minutes, until lightly golden brown all over.

6 Remove with a slotted spoon, drain on kitchen paper and keep warm while frying the remainder. Garnish with watercress or mizuna. Serve with lime wedges and the mayonnaise.

Herbed Fish Croquettes

Deep-fry with clean oil every time as the fish will flavour the oil and taint any other foods later fried in it.

Serves 4
450g/1lb plaice or flounder fillets
300ml/½ pint/1¼ cups milk
450g/1lb cooked potatoes
1 fennel bulb, finely chopped
1 garlic clove, finely chopped

45ml/3 tbsp chopped
   fresh parsley
2 eggs
15g/½oz/1 tbsp unsalted
   (sweet) butter
225g/8oz/2 cups white
   breadcrumbs
30ml/2 tbsp sesame seeds
vegetable oil, for deep-frying
salt and ground black pepper

1 Put the fish fillets in a large pan, add the milk and bring just to the boil. Lower the heat, cover and poach gently for about 15 minutes, until the fish flakes easily with the tip of a knife. Remove the fillets with a slotted spoon and set aside until cool enough to handle. Reserve the milk.

2 Remove the skin and any bones from the fish and coarsely flake the flesh. Put the fish, potatoes, fennel, garlic, parsley, eggs and butter in a food processor fitted with a metal blade and process until thoroughly combined.

3 Add 30ml/2 tbsp of the reserved cooking milk, season to taste with salt and pepper and process briefly again.

4 Scrape the fish mixture into a bowl, cover with clear film (plastic wrap) and chill in the refrigerator for about 30 minutes.

5 Using your hands shape the fish mixture into 20 croquettes. Mix together the breadcrumbs and sesame seeds on a shallow plate. Roll the croquettes in the breadcrumb mixture to form a good coating.

6 Heat the oil in a large heavy pan to 180°C/350°F, or until a cube of day-old bread browns in 30 seconds. Deep-fry the croquettes, in batches, for about 4 minutes until golden brown. Drain well on kitchen paper and serve immediately.

Croquettes Energy 625kcal/2627kJ; Protein 35.9g; Carbohydrate 63.3g, of which sugars 4.3g; Fat 27.3g, of which saturates 5.8g; Cholesterol 246mg; Calcium 252mg; Fibre 4.6g; Sodium 681mg.
Goujons Energy 482kcal/1997kJ; Protein 8.1g; Carbohydrate 24.5g, of which sugars 1.6g; Fat 39.7g, of which saturates 4.9g; Cholesterol 31mg; Calcium 126mg; Fibre 0.1g; Sodium 486mg.

Pan-fried Garlic Sardines

Lightly fry a sliced garlic clove to garnish the fish. This dish could also be made with sprats or fresh anchovies, if available.

4 garlic cloves
finely grated rind of 2 lemons
30ml/2 tbsp chopped
   fresh parsley
salt and ground black pepper

Serves 4
1.2kg/2½lb fresh sardines
30ml/2 tbsp olive oil

For the tomato bread
4 large potatoes
1 tbsp butter

1 First, scale the sardines. Hold each fish by the tail under cold running water and run your other hand all along the body from tail to head to scrape off the scales. Cut off the fish heads if you like. Slit open the belly of each fish, using a sharp knife, and remove the guts with your fingers. Rinse the body cavities well under cold running water and pat dry with kitchen paper.

2 Heat the olive oil in a heavy frying pan over medium-low heat. Add the garlic cloves and cook, stirring frequently, for 1–2 minutes, until softened.

3 Add the sardines to the pan and cook, turning once, for 4–5 minutes until light golden brown. Sprinkle the lemon rind and parsley over the fish and season to taste with salt and black pepper.

4 Cut the potatoes into small chunks. Boil for 15 minutes, or until soft. Drain the water, keeping the potatoes in the pan. Add the butter and stir with a wooden spoon the mixture is smooth. Serve with the sardines and season with black pepper.

> ### Cook's Tips
> • Scaling the sardines is, without question, a very messy and time-consuming business. However, the fish are so much nicer to eat when scaled that it is worth the effort. (Clear the discarded scales from the sink afterwards.)

Grilled Salmon Steaks with Fennel

Fennel grows wild all over the south of Italy where this dish originated. Its mild aniseed flavour goes well with fish.

5ml/1 tsp fennel seeds
45ml/3 tbsp olive oil
4 salmon steaks of the same
   thickness (about 700g/1½lb)
salt and ground black pepper
lemon wedges, to garnish

Serves 4
juice of 1 lemon
45ml/3 tbsp chopped fresh
   fennel, or the green fronds from
   the top of a fennel bulb

1 Combine the lemon juice, chopped fennel and fennel seeds with the olive oil in a non-metallic dish. Add the salmon steaks, turning them to coat them with the marinade. Sprinkle with salt and pepper. Cover with clear film (plastic wrap) and place in the refrigerator to marinate for about 2 hours.

2 Preheat the grill (broiler). Drain the fish and reserve the marinade. Place the salmon steaks in one layer on a grill (broiler) pan or shallow baking tray. Grill (broil) about 10cm/4in from the heat source for 3–4 minutes.

3 Turn the steaks over and spoon the remaining marinade over them. Grill for 3–4 minutes, or until the edges begin to brown. Serve immediately, garnished with lemon wedges.

> ### Cook's Tips
> • If you like, remove the skin from the salmon steaks before serving. Simply insert the prongs of a fork between the flesh and the skin at one end and roll the skin around the prongs in a fluid action.
> • Take care not to overcook the salmon. Although it is an oily fish, the flesh dries out very easily when subjected to fierce heat. If you're going to cook on the barbecue, raise the grill rack well above the coals before starting.

Sardines Energy 513kcal/2149kJ; Protein 47.4g; Carbohydrate 27.9g, of which sugars 4.5g; Fat 24.1g, of which saturates 5.8g; Cholesterol 0mg; Calcium 279mg; Fibre 2g; Sodium 504mg.
Salmon Energy 395kcal/1639kJ; Protein 35.8g; Carbohydrate 0.8g, of which sugars 0.8g; Fat 27.6g, of which saturates 4.5g; Cholesterol 88mg; Calcium 47mg; Fibre 1.1g; Sodium 84mg.

Stuffed Fish Rolls

Plaice or flounder fillets are a good choice for families because they are economical, easy to cook and free of bones.

Serves 4

1 courgette (zucchini), grated
2 carrots, grated
60ml/4 tbsp fresh wholemeal (whole-wheat) breadcrumbs
15ml/1 tbsp lime or lemon juice
4 plaice or flounder fillets
salt and ground black pepper
new potatoes, to serve

1 Preheat the oven to 200°C/400°F/Gas 6. Mix together the courgette and carrots in a bowl. Stir in the breadcrumbs and lime juice and season with salt and pepper.

2 Lay the fish fillets, skin-side up, on a board and divide the stuffing among them, spreading it evenly.

3 Roll up to enclose the stuffing and place in an ovenproof dish. Cover and bake for about 30 minutes, or until the fish flakes easily. Serve immediately with new potatoes.

Cook's Tip
Flat fish, such as plaice and flounder, have one light- and one dark-skinned side. Most people consider the darker skin to be unappetizing and many dislike any sort of skin. The skin is very easy to remove. Make a small cut between the skin and the flesh at the tail end of the fillet, then dip your fingers in salt to stop them from slipping, take a firm hold of the skin and simply pull it away from the flesh in one piece. Spread the filling on to the side where the skin was.

Variation
Substitute 115g/4oz/1 cup finely chopped cooked, peeled prawns or drained, canned crab meat for the carrots to create a more sophisticated version of this dish.

Mackerel Kebabs with Parsley

Oily fish, such as mackerel, are ideal for grilling as they cook quickly and need no extra oil.

Serves 4

450g/1lb mackerel fillets
finely grated rind and juice of 1 lemon
45ml/3 tbsp chopped fresh parsley
12 cherry tomatoes
8 pitted black olives
salt and ground black pepper
boiled rice or noodles and green salad, to serve

1 Cut the fish into 4cm/1½ in chunks and place in a non-metallic bowl with half the lemon rind and juice and half the parsley and season with salt and pepper. Cover the bowl with clear film (plastic wrap) and leave to marinate in a cool place for about 30 minutes.

2 Preheat the grill (broiler). Thread the chunks of fish on to eight long wooden or metal skewers, alternating them with the cherry tomatoes and olives. Grill (broil) the kebabs, turning occasionally, for 3–4 minutes, until the fish is cooked.

3 Mix the remaining lemon rind and juice with the remaining parsley in a small bowl, then season to taste with salt and pepper. Make a bed of plain boiled rice or noodles on each of four warmed serving plates and place two kebabs on each. Serve immediately with a green salad.

Cook's Tips
• If you are using wooden kebab skewers, it is a good idea to soak them in cold water for 30 minutes to prevent them from charring during cooking.
• These kebabs are also ideal for cooking on the barbecue. Serve with baked potatoes or crusty bread and salad.
• If you are going to marinate the fish for longer than 30 minutes, place it in the refrigerator. Otherwise, simply leave it in a cool place.

Fish Rolls Energy 139kcal/588kJ; Protein 15.5g; Carbohydrate 16.5g, of which sugars 5g; Fat 1.7g, of which saturates 0.3g; Cholesterol 32mg; Calcium 78mg; Fibre 2g; Sodium 217mg.
Mackerel Energy 265kcal/1100kJ; Protein 21.7g; Carbohydrate 1.5g, of which sugars 1.5g; Fat 19.1g, of which saturates 3.9g; Cholesterol 61mg; Calcium 44mg; Fibre 1.2g; Sodium 219mg.

Salmon Pasta with Parsley Sauce

The parsley sauce is prepared and added at the last moment to the salmon mixture and does not have to be cooked separately.

Serves 4
450g/1lb salmon fillet
225g/8oz/2 cups pasta, such
   as penne

175g/6oz cherry tomatoes, halved
150ml/¼ pint/⅔ cup crème
   fraîche or sour cream
45ml/3 tbsp finely chopped
   fresh parsley
finely grated rind of ½ orange
salt and ground black pepper

1 Skin the salmon if this has not already been done by your fish supplier and cut the flesh into bitesize pieces. Spread out the pieces of fish on a heatproof plate and cover with foil.

2 Bring a large pan of salted water to the boil, add the pasta and bring back to the boil. Place the plate of salmon on top of the pan and cook for 10–12 minutes, until the pasta is just tender and the salmon is cooked.

3 Set the plate of salmon aside, then drain the pasta and return it to the pan. Add the tomatoes and salmon to the pasta and toss well.

4 Mix together the crème fraîche or sour cream, parsley and orange rind in a bowl and season with pepper to taste. Add the parsley sauce to the salmon and pasta, toss again and serve hot or leave to cool to room temperature.

Variations
• Sea trout, also known as salmon trout, would also be beautifully complemented by the parsley sauce in this recipe. Other, perhaps less obvious substitutes could be gurnard (US sea robin) fillets.
• You could also try using trout fillets and substitute grated lemon rind for the orange.

Cod with Spiced Red Lentils

This is a very tasty, filling and economical dish, with the added bonus of being a healthy option.

Serves 4
175g/6oz/¾ cup red lentils
1.25ml/¼ tsp ground turmeric
600ml/1 pint/2½ cups fish stock
450g/1lb cod fillets
30ml/2 tbsp vegetable oil

7.5ml/1½ tsp cumin seeds
15ml/1 tbsp grated fresh
   root ginger
2.5ml/½ tsp cayenne pepper
15ml/1 tbsp lemon or lime juice
30ml/2 tbsp chopped fresh
   coriander (cilantro)
pinch of salt, to taste
fresh coriander leaves and lemon
   or lime wedges, to garnish

1 Put the lentils in a pan with the turmeric and fish stock. Bring to the boil, then lower the heat, cover with a tight-fitting lid and simmer for 20–25 minutes, until the lentils are just tender. Remove from the heat, season with salt and set aside.

2 Meanwhile, skin the cod fillets if this has not already been done by your supplier and cut the flesh into large chunks with a sharp knife. Place the pieces on a plate, cover with clear film (plastic wrap) and store in the refrigerator until required.

3 Heat the oil in a small, heavy frying pan over medium-low heat. Add the cumin seeds and cook, stirring occasionally, until they begin to pop and give off their aroma, then add the grated ginger and cayenne pepper. Stir-fry the spices for a few seconds more, then pour the mixture on to the lentils. Add the lemon or lime juice and the chopped coriander and stir them gently into the mixture.

4 Lay the pieces of cod on top of the lentils, cover the pan and then cook gently over low heat for 10–15 minutes, or until the fish is tender and cooked through.

5 Spoon the cod and lentil mixture on to warmed individual plates. Sprinkle the the whole coriander leaves over the top and garnish each serving with one or two lemon or lime wedges. Serve immediately.

Salmon Energy 469kcal/1971kJ; Protein 31.2g; Carbohydrate 45.4g, of which sugars 5g; Fat 19.3g, of which saturates 6.1g; Cholesterol 56mg; Calcium 100mg; Fibre 2.8g; Sodium 75mg.
Cod Energy 279kcal/1174kJ; Protein 31g; Carbohydrate 24.6g, of which sugars 1.1g; Fat 6.9g, of which saturates 0.9g; Cholesterol 52mg; Calcium 33mg; Fibre 2.2g; Sodium 83mg.

Golden Fish Pie

This lovely light pie with a crumpled filo pastry topping makes a delicious lunch or supper dish.

Serves 4–6
675g/1½lb white fish fillets
300ml/½ pint/1¼ cups milk
½ onion, thinly sliced
1 bay leaf
6 black peppercorns
115g/4oz/1 cup cooked peeled prawns (shrimp)

115g/4oz/½ cup butter
50g/2oz/½ cup plain (all-purpose) flour
300ml/½ pint/1¼ cups single (light) cream
75g/3oz/¾ cup grated Gruyère cheese
1 bunch watercress, leaves only, chopped
5ml/1 tsp Dijon mustard
5 sheets filo pastry
salt and ground black pepper

1 Place the fish in a pan, pour in the milk and add the onion, bay leaf and peppercorns. Bring to the boil, lower the heat, cover with a lid and simmer for 10–12 minutes, until the fish is almost tender. Lift out the fish with a slotted spatula and place on a chopping board. Strain and reserve the cooking liquid.

2 Remove the skin and any bones from the fish, then coarsely flake the flesh and place in a shallow, ovenproof dish. Sprinkle the prawns over the fish.

3 Melt 50g/2oz/4 tbsp of the butter in a pan. Stir in the flour and cook, stirring constantly, for 1 minute. Stir in the reserved cooking liquid and cream. Bring to the boil, stirring, then simmer for 2–3 minutes, until thickened. Remove from the heat and stir in the Gruyère, watercress and mustard. Season with salt and pepper. Pour the mixture over the fish and leave to cool.

4 Preheat the oven to 190°C/375°F/Gas 5, then melt the remaining butter. Brush one sheet of filo pastry with a little melted butter, then crumple up loosely and place on top of the filling. Repeat with the remaining filo sheets and melted butter until they are all used up and the pie is completely covered. Bake for 25–30 minutes, until the pastry is golden and crisp. Serve immediately.

Special Fish Pie

This fish pie is colourful, healthy and best of all, it is very simple to make.

Serves 4
350g/12oz haddock fillet
30ml/2 tbsp cornflour (cornstarch)
115g/4oz/1 cup cooked peeled prawns (shrimp)
200g/7oz can corn, drained
75g/3oz/scant 1 cup frozen peas

150ml/¼ pint/¾ cup skimmed milk
150ml/¼ pint/¾ cup low-fat fromage frais (farmer's cheese)
75g/3oz/1½ cups fresh wholemeal (whole-wheat) breadcrumbs
40g/1½ oz/generous ¼ cup grated reduced-fat Cheddar cheese
salt and ground black pepper
fresh vegetables, to serve

1 Preheat the oven to 190°C/375°F/Gas 5. Skin the haddock fillet if this has not already been done by your fish supplier and cut the flesh into bitesize pieces. Toss the pieces of fish in the cornflour to coat evenly.

2 Place the fish, prawns, corn and peas in an ovenproof dish. Beat together the milk and fromage frais in a bowl and season with salt and pepper. Pour the mixture into the dish.

3 Mix together the breadcrumbs and grated cheese, then spoon evenly over the top, pressing down gently with the back of the spoon.

4 Bake for 25–30 minutes, or until the topping is golden brown. Serve hot with fresh vegetables.

> **Variations**
> • For a slightly more economical version of this dish, omit the prawns (shrimp) and increase the quantity of haddock fillet to 450g/1lb.
> • Substitute smoked haddock fillet for half the fresh fish.
> • Use frozen or drained canned broad (fava) beans instead of the peas.

Golden Fish Energy 344kcal/1442kJ; Protein 32g; Carbohydrate 17.5g, of which sugars 3.8g; Fat 16.4g, of which saturates 9g; Cholesterol 129mg; Calcium 239mg; Fibre 0.8g; Sodium 246mg.
Special Fish Energy 329kcal/1394kJ; Protein 34.1g; Carbohydrate 41.2g, of which sugars 10g; Fat 4.3g, of which saturates 1.7g; Cholesterol 94mg; Calcium 228mg; Fibre 2g; Sodium 490mg.

Fishcakes

Home-made fish cakes are an underrated food which bear little resemblance to the store-bought type.

Serves 4

450g/1lb mixed white and smoked fish fillets, such as haddock or cod, flaked
450g/1lb cooked, mashed potatoes
25g/1oz/2 tbsp butter, diced
45ml/3 tbsp chopped fresh parsley
1 egg, separated
1 egg, beaten
about 50g/2oz/1 cup fine white breadcrumbs made with day-old bread
salt and pepper
vegetable oil, for pan-frying

1 Place the fish in a large pan, season with salt and pepper and pour in water just to cover. Bring to the boil, then lower the heat, cover and simmer for about 15 minutes, until the flesh flakes easily with the tip of a knife. Remove the fish with a slotted spatula and leave until cool enough to handle. Discard the cooking liquid.

2 Remove and discard the skin and any bones from the fish and flake the flesh. Place the potatoes in a bowl and beat in the fish, butter, parsley and egg yolk. Season to taste with pepper.

3 Divide the fish mixture into eight equal portions, then, with floured hands, form each into a flat patty. Beat the remaining egg white with the whole egg. Dip each fish cake first into the beaten egg, then in breadcrumbs.

4 Heat the oil in a frying pan over a medium heat. Add the fish cakes and cook for 3–5 minutes on each side, until crisp and golden. Serve immediately.

> **Cook's Tip**
> Make smaller fishcakes to serve as an appetizer with a salad garnish. For a more luxurious version, make them with cooked fresh salmon or drained, canned red or pink salmon.

Fish & Chips

The traditional British combination of battered fish and thick-cut chips is served with lemon wedges.

Serves 4

115g/4oz/1 cup self-raising (self-rising) flour
150ml/¼ pint/⅔ cup water
675g/1½lb potatoes
675g/1½lb skinned cod fillet, cut into four
vegetable oil, for deep-frying
salt and ground black pepper
lemon wedges, to serve

1 Stir the flour and a pinch of salt together in a bowl, then form a well in the centre. Gradually pour into the water, whisking in the flour to make a smooth batter. Leave to stand for 30 minutes.

2 Cut the potatoes into strips about 1cm/½ in wide and 5cm/2in long. Place the potatoes in a colander, rinse in cold water, then drain and dry them well with kitchen paper.

3 Heat the oil in a deep-fat fryer or large heavy pan to 150°C/300°F, or until a cube of day-old bread browns in 50 seconds. Using the wire basket, lower the potatoes, in batches, into the oil and cook for 5–6 minutes, shaking the basket occasionally until the potatoes are soft but not browned. Remove the chips (French fries) from the oil and drain them thoroughly on kitchen paper.

4 Heat the oil in the fryer to 190°C/375°F, or until a cube of day-old bread browns in 30 seconds. Season the fish with salt and pepper. Stir the batter, then dip the pieces of fish in turn into it, allowing the excess to drain off.

5 Working in two batches if necessary, lower the fish into the oil and fry for 6–8 minutes, until crisp and brown. Drain the fish on kitchen paper and keep warm.

6 Add the chips, in batches, to the oil and cook them for 2–3 minutes, until golden and crisp. Keep hot until ready to serve, then sprinkle with salt and serve with the fish, accompanied by lemon wedges.

Fishcakes Energy 399kcal/1670kJ; Protein 27.5g; Carbohydrate 28.2g, of which sugars 2.1g; Fat 20.4g, of which saturates 5.6g; Cholesterol 160mg; Calcium 71mg; Fibre 2g; Sodium 252mg.
Fish & Chips Energy 820kcal/3429kJ; Protein 32.6g; Carbohydrate 71.2g, of which sugars 2.9g; Fat 40.5g, of which saturates 13g; Cholesterol 0mg; Calcium 132mg; Fibre 4.6g; Sodium 329mg.

Prawn & Mint Salad

The spices used to make the dressing gives the prawns a refreshing and fiery flavour.

Serves 4

12 large raw prawns (shrimp)
15g/½ oz/1 tbsp unsalted (sweet) butter
15ml/1 tbsp Thai fish sauce
juice of 1 lime
45ml/3 tbsp thin coconut milk
2.5cm/1in piece of fresh root ginger, peeled and grated
5ml/1 tsp caster (superfine) sugar
1 garlic clove, crushed
2 fresh red chillies, seeded and finely chopped
30ml/2 tbsp fresh mint leaves
ground black pepper
225g/8oz light green lettuce leaves, such as round (butterhead), to serve

1 Pull off the heads from the prawns and peel them, leaving the tails intact. Make a small cut along the back of each prawn and remove the dark vein with the point of the knife.

2 Melt the butter in a large frying pan over medium heat. Add the prawns and cook, turning and tossing frequently, for about 3 minutes, until they turn pink.

3 Mix the Thai fish sauce, lime juice, coconut milk, ginger, sugar, garlic, chillies and pepper together in a large bowl.

4 Add the warm prawns to the sauce and toss well, then add the mint leaves and toss again.

5 Make a bed of green lettuce leaves on each of four individual plates and divide the prawns and sauce among them. Serve the salads immediately.

> **Cook's Tip**
> For a really tropical touch, garnish this flavoursome salad with some shavings of fresh coconut (made using a vegetable peeler) or with grated papaya. Use slightly unripe fruit and peel and remove the seeds before grating.

Chilli Prawns

This delightful, spicy combination makes a lovely light main course for an informal supper.

Serves 3–4

45ml/3 tbsp olive oil
2 shallots, chopped
2 garlic cloves, chopped
1 fresh red chilli, chopped
450g/1lb ripe tomatoes, peeled, seeded and chopped
15ml/1 tbsp tomato purée (paste)
1 bay leaf
1 fresh thyme sprig
90ml/6 tbsp dry white wine
450g/1lb/4 cups cooked peeled large prawns (shrimp)
salt and ground black pepper
coarsely torn fresh basil leaves, to garnish

1 Heat the olive oil in a pan over low heat. Add the shallots, garlic and chilli and cook, stirring occasionally, for about 5 minutes, until the shallots have softened and the garlic starts to brown.

2 Increase the heat to medium, add the tomatoes, tomato purée, bay leaf, thyme sprig and wine and season to taste with salt and pepper. Bring to the boil, then lower the heat and simmer gently, stirring occasionally, for about 10 minutes, until the sauce has thickened. Remove and discard the bay leaf and thyme sprig.

3 Stir the prawns into the sauce and heat through for a few minutes. Taste and adjust the seasoning if necessary. Sprinkle the basil leaves over the top and serve immediately.

> **Cook's Tip**
> Avoid buying frozen cooked prawns (shrimp), if possible, as they often have a soggy texture and poor flavour, especially if they have been peeled before freezing. If freshly cooked prawns are not available, then consider using raw prawns and cook them in the sauce a little longer or pan-fry or boil them until they change colour before adding them in step 3.

Prawn Salad Energy 76kcal/319kJ; Protein 9.3g; Carbohydrate 1.5g, of which sugars 1.5g; Fat 3.7g, of which saturates 2.1g; Cholesterol 106mg; Calcium 59mg; Fibre 0.5g; Sodium 132mg.
Chilli Prawns Energy 202kcal/845kJ; Protein 21g; Carbohydrate 5.4g, of which sugars 5g; Fat 9.3g, of which saturates 1.4g; Cholesterol 219mg; Calcium 104mg; Fibre 1.5g; Sodium 234mg.

Scallops with Ginger

Scallops are at their best in winter. Rich and creamy, this dish is very simple to make and quite delicious.

Serves 4
8–12 shelled scallops
40g/1½oz/3 tbsp butter
2.5cm/1in piece fresh root ginger, finely chopped
1 bunch of spring onions (scallions), sliced diagonally
60ml/4 tbsp white vermouth
250ml/8fl oz/1 cup crème fraîche
salt and ground black pepper
chopped fresh parsley, to garnish

1 Remove the white muscle opposite the coral on each scallop if this has not already been done by your supplier. Separate the coral from the white part and cut the white part of the scallop in half horizontally. Reserve the corals.

2 Melt the butter in a frying pan over medium heat. Add the scallops, including the corals, and sauté for about 2 minutes until lightly browned. Take care not to overcook the scallops as this will toughen them.

3 Lift out the scallops with a slotted spoon and transfer to a warmed serving dish. Keep warm.

4 Add the ginger and spring onions to the pan and stir-fry for 2 minutes. Pour in the vermouth and leave to bubble until it has almost evaporated. Stir in the crème fraîche and cook for a few minutes until the sauce has thickened. Season to taste with salt and pepper.

5 Pour the sauce over the scallops, sprinkle with parsley and serve immediately.

> **Cook's Tip**
> *The orange-coloured coral of the scallop is the roe and this, with the round, white adductor muscle, this comprises the edible part. In Europe the coral is regarded as a delicacy, although in the United States it is usually discarded.*

Seafood Pilaff

This one-pan dish makes a satisfying meal. For a special occasion, use dry white wine instead of orange juice.

Serves 4
10ml/2 tsp olive oil
250g/9oz/1⅓ cups long grain rice
5ml/1 tsp ground turmeric
1 fresh red (bell) pepper, seeded and diced
1 small onion, finely chopped
2 courgettes (zucchini), sliced
150g/5oz button (white) mushrooms, halved
350ml/12fl oz/1½ cups fish or chicken stock
150ml/¼ pint/⅔ cup orange juice
350g/12oz white fish fillets
12 fresh mussels, scrubbed and debearded
salt and ground black pepper
grated rind of 1 orange, to garnish

1 Heat the oil in a large non-stick frying pan over low heat. Add the rice and turmeric and cook, stirring frequently, for about 1 minute.

2 Add the red pepper, onion, courgettes and mushrooms and cook, stirring constantly, for 1 minute more, then increase the heat to medium, stir in the stock and orange juice and bring to the boil.

3 Lower the heat and add the fish. Cover with a tight-fitting lid and simmer gently for about 15 minutes, until the rice is tender and the liquid has been absorbed.

4 Stir in the mussels, re-cover the pan and cook for about 5 minutes until the shells have opened. Discard any mussels that remain closed. Adjust the seasoning, sprinkle with orange rind and serve immediately.

> **Variation**
> *You can use cooked, shelled mussels, available from the chiller cabinets in supermarkets, instead of live. Add them in step 4 and simply heat through before serving.*

Scallops Energy 392kcal/1621kJ; Protein 13.6g; Carbohydrate 4.5g, of which sugars 2.5g; Fat 34.1g, of which saturates 22.4g; Cholesterol 115mg; Calcium 63mg; Fibre 0.4g; Sodium 168mg.
Pilaff Energy 394kcal/1663kJ; Protein 28.7g; Carbohydrate 59g, of which sugars 12.5g; Fat 6.3g, of which saturates 0.5g; Cholesterol 46mg; Calcium 620mg; Fibre 2.3g; Sodium 115mg.

Chicken with Lemon & Herbs

Chicken thighs tend to be overlooked when people are buying portions, yet the meat is full of flavour and two thighs will adequately serve one person.

Serves 2
50g/2oz/4 tbsp butter
2 spring onions, (scallions) white parts only, finely chopped

15ml/1 tbsp chopped fresh tarragon
15ml/1 tbsp chopped fresh fennel
juice of 1 lemon
4 chicken thighs
salt and ground black pepper
lemon slices and fresh herb sprigs, to garnish

1 Preheat the grill (broiler) to medium. Melt the butter in a small pan over low heat. Add the spring onions, tarragon, fennel and lemon juice and season with salt and pepper. Cook, stirring constantly, for 1 minute, then remove the pan from the heat.

2 Brush the chicken thighs generously with the herb mixture, then grill (broil), basting frequently with the herb mixture, for 10–12 minutes.

3 Turn the chicken over and baste again, then cook for a further 10–12 minutes, or until the chicken juices run clear when the thickest part of the thigh is pierced with the point of a knife.

4 Serve the chicken garnished with lemon slices and herb sprigs and accompanied by any remaining herb mixture.

> **Cook's Tip**
> *Tarragon has a natural affinity with chicken. It is intensely aromatic with a hint of aniseed and so should be used sparingly. Make sure you buy French tarragon with its delicate leaves and fine flavour. Russian tarragon is virtually inedible. Fennel also has a strong aniseed flavour, so it too should be used with discretion.*

Roast Chicken with Celeriac

Celeriac and brown breadcrumbs give the stuffing an unusual and delicious twist.

Serves 4
1.6kg/3½lb chicken
15g/½oz/1 tbsp butter

For the stuffing
450g/1lb celeriac, chopped
25g/1oz/2 tbsp butter
3 rashers (strips) bacon, chopped

1 onion, finely chopped
leaves from 1 fresh thyme sprig, chopped
leaves from 1 small fresh tarragon sprig, chopped
30ml/2 tbsp chopped fresh parsley
75g/3oz/1½ cups fresh brown breadcrumbs
dash of Worcestershire sauce
1 egg
salt and ground black pepper

1 To make the stuffing, cook the celeriac in a pan of boiling water until tender. Drain well and chop finely.

2 Melt the butter in a heavy pan over low heat. Add the bacon and onion and cook, stirring occasionally, for 5–7 minutes, until the onion is softened but not coloured.

3 Stir in the celeriac, thyme, tarragon and parsley and cook, stirring occasionally, for 2–3 minutes. Meanwhile, preheat the oven to 200°C/400°F/Gas 6.

4 Remove the pan from the heat and stir in the fresh breadcrumbs, Worcestershire sauce and sufficient egg to bind the mixture. Season with salt and pepper. Use this mixture to stuff the neck end of the chicken. Season the chicken all over with salt and pepper and then rub the butter into the skin with your fingertips.

5 Place the chicken in a roasting pan and roast, basting occasionally with the cooking juices, for 1¼–1½ hours, until the juices run clear when the thickest part of the leg is pierced with the point of a sharp knife. Turn off the oven, prop the door open slightly and leave the chicken to rest for about 10 minutes before removing from the oven and carving.

Roast Chicken Energy 507kcal/2116kJ; Protein 43.6g; Carbohydrate 16.8g, of which sugars 2.4g; Fat 30g, of which saturates 11.6g; Cholesterol 233mg; Calcium 99mg; Fibre 1.9g; Sodium 692mg.
Lemon Chicken Energy 406kcal/1692kJ; Protein 42.1g; Carbohydrate 0.5g, of which sugars 0.4g; Fat 26.2g, of which saturates 14.7g; Cholesterol 263mg; Calcium 23mg; Fibre 0.3g; Sodium 333mg.

Chicken with Peppers

This colourful and tasty dish comes from the south of Italy, where sweet peppers are plentiful.

Serves 4

1.5kg/3lb chicken, cut into
    serving pieces
90ml/6 tbsp olive oil
2 red onions, thinly sliced
2 garlic cloves, finely chopped
small piece of dried chilli,
    crumbled (optional)
120ml/4fl oz/½ cup dry
    white wine
3 large (bell) peppers (red, yellow
    or green), seeded and cut
    into strips
2 tomatoes, fresh or canned,
    peeled and chopped
45g/3 tbsp chopped fresh parsley
salt and ground black pepper

1 Trim any visible fat off the chicken with a sharp knife and remove all excess skin.

2 Heat half the oil in a large heavy pan or flameproof casserole over low heat. Add the onions and cook, stirring occasionally, for 5–7 minutes, until softened but not coloured. Transfer them to a plate.

3 Add the remaining oil to the pan and increase the heat to medium. Add the chicken pieces and cook, turning frequently, for 6–8 minutes, until browned on all sides. Return the onions to the pan and add the garlic and dried chilli, if using.

4 Pour in the wine and cook until it has reduced by about half. Add the peppers and stir well to coat. Season to taste with salt and pepper and cook for 3–4 minutes. Stir in the tomatoes, lower the heat, cover the pan with a tight-fitting lid and cook, stirring occasionally, for 25–30 minutes, until the peppers are soft and the chicken is cooked through. Stir in the chopped parsley and serve immediately.

Cook's Tip
For a more elegant version of this dish to serve at a dinner party, use skinless, boneless chicken breast portions.

Golden Parmesan Chicken

Served cold with the garlic mayonnaise, these morsels of chicken make fabulous picnic food.

Serves 4

4 skinless boneless chicken
    breast portions
75g/3oz/1½ cups fresh
    white breadcrumbs
40g/1½oz/½ cup finely grated
    Parmesan cheese
30ml/2 tbsp chopped
    fresh parsley

2 eggs, lightly beaten
50g/2oz/4 tbsp butter, melted
salt and ground black pepper
green salad, to serve

For the garlic mayonnaise

120ml/4fl oz/½ cup good-
    quality mayonnaise
120ml/4fl oz/½ cup fromage
    frais (farmer's cheese)
1–2 garlic cloves, crushed

1 Using a sharp knife, cut each chicken portion into four or five large pieces. Mix together the breadcrumbs, grated Parmesan cheese and parsley in a shallow dish and season with salt and pepper.

2 Dip the chicken pieces in the beaten egg, then into the breadcrumb mixture. Place in a single layer on a baking sheet and chill in the refrigerator for at least 30 minutes.

3 Meanwhile, make the garlic mayonnaise. Mix together the mayonnaise, fromage frais and garlic and season with pepper to taste. Spoon the mayonnaise into a small serving bowl, cover with clear film (plastic wrap) and chill in the refrigerator until ready to serve.

4 Preheat the oven to 180°C/350°F/Gas 4. Drizzle the melted butter over the chicken pieces and cook in the oven for about 20 minutes, until crisp and golden. Serve the chicken immediately with a crisp green salad and the garlic mayonnaise for dipping. Alternatively, transfer the chicken to a rack, using tongs, and leave to cool. Store in the refrigerator until required, then serve at room temperature with a green salad and the garlic mayonnaise.

With Peppers Energy 512kcal/2127kJ; Protein 31.9g; Carbohydrate 17.2g, of which sugars 15g; Fat 33.3g, of which saturates 8g; Cholesterol 130mg; Calcium 71mg; Fibre 4.4g; Sodium 128mg.
Golden Chicken Energy 625kcal/2608kJ; Protein 48g; Carbohydrate 17.2g, of which sugars 3g; Fat 41.1g, of which saturates 13.3g; Cholesterol 260mg; Calcium 199mg; Fibre 0.5g; Sodium 598mg.

Chicken in Green Sauce

Slow, gentle cooking makes the chicken in this dish very succulent and tender.

Serves 4
25g/1oz/2 tbsp butter
15ml/1 tbsp olive oil
4 chicken portions (legs, breast portions or quarters)
1 small onion, finely chopped
150ml/¼ pint/⅔ cup medium-bodied dry white wine
150ml/¼ pint/⅔ cup chicken stock
leaves from 2 fresh thyme sprigs and 2 fresh tarragon sprigs
175g/6oz watercress, leaves removed, or baby spinach leaves, trimmed
150ml/¼ pint/⅔ cup double (heavy) cream
salt and ground black pepper
watercress leaves or mizuna, to garnish

1 Heat the butter and oil in a frying pan over medium heat. Add the chicken portions and cook, turning frequently, for 8–10 minutes, until browned all over. Transfer the chicken to a plate using a slotted spoon and keep warm in the oven.

2 Lower the heat, add the onion to the pan and cook, stirring occasionally, for 5–7 minutes, until softened but not coloured. Stir in the wine, increase the heat to medium and bring to the boil. Boil for 2–3 minutes, then add the stock and bring the mixture back to the boil.

3 Return the chicken to the pan, lower the heat, cover with a tight-fitting lid and simmer very gently for about 30 minutes, until the chicken juices run clear when the thickest part of the meat is pierced with the point of a knife. Transfer the chicken to a warm dish, cover and keep warm.

4 Boil the cooking juices hard until they are reduced to about 60ml/4 tbsp. Add the thyme, tarragon and watercress or spinach leaves and stir in the cream. Simmer over medium heat until slightly thickened.

5 Return the chicken to the pan, season to taste with salt and pepper and heat through for a few minutes. Transfer to warmed serving plates, garnish with watercress or mizuna and serve.

Coronation Chicken

Created in 1953 in honour of the coronation of HM Queen Elizabeth II, this cold chicken dish with a mild, curry-flavoured sauce is ideal for summer lunch parties and picnics.

Serves 8
½ lemon
2.25kg/5lb chicken
1 onion, quartered
1 carrot, quartered
1 large bouquet garni
8 black peppercorns, crushed
pinch of salt
fresh watercress or parsley sprigs, to garnish

For the sauce
1 small onion, chopped
15g/½oz/1 tbsp butter
15ml/1 tbsp curry paste
15ml/1 tbsp tomato purée (paste)
120ml/4fl oz/½ cup red wine
1 bay leaf
juice of ½ lemon, or to taste
10–15ml/2–3 tsp apricot jam
300ml/½ pint/1¼ cups mayonnaise
120ml/4fl oz/½ cup whipping cream, whipped
salt and ground black pepper

1 Put the lemon half in the chicken cavity, then place the chicken in a pan that it just fits. Add the onion, carrot, bouquet garni, peppercorns and salt.

2 Add sufficient water to come two-thirds of the way up the chicken and bring to the boil, then lower the heat, cover and simmer for about 1½ hours, until the chicken juices run clear.

3 Transfer the chicken to a large bowl, pour the cooking liquid over it and leave to cool. When cool, transfer the chicken to a board. Remove the skin and bones and chop the flesh.

4 To make the sauce, cook the onion in the butter until soft. Add the curry paste, tomato purée, wine, bay leaf and lemon juice, then cook for 10 minutes. Add the jam; sieve and cool.

5 Beat the sauce mixture into the mayonnaise. Fold in the cream, season to taste with salt and pepper and add the lemon juice, then stir in with the chicken. Garnish and serve.

In green sauce Energy 502kcal/2089kJ; Protein 44.5g; Carbohydrate 3.3g, of which sugars 3g; Fat 32.1g, of which saturates 17.3g; Cholesterol 227mg; Calcium 114mg; Fibre 0.9g; Sodium 215mg.
Coronation Energy 480kcal/1994kJ; Protein 30.9g; Carbohydrate 2.8g, of which sugars 2.5g; Fat 37.3g, of which saturates 9.4g; Cholesterol 135mg; Calcium 22mg; Fibre 0.2g; Sodium 265mg.

Stoved Chicken

"Stoved" is derived from the French *étouffer*, meaning to cook in a covered pot.

Serves 4

1kg/2lb potatoes, cut into
*   5mm/¼in slices*
2 large onions, thinly sliced
15ml/1 tbsp chopped fresh thyme

25g/1oz/2 tbsp butter
15ml/1 tbsp sunflower oil
2 large bacon rashers
*   (strips), chopped*
4 large chicken portions, halved
1 bay leaf
600ml/1 pint/2½ cups chicken
*   stock*
salt and ground black pepper

1 Preheat the oven to 150°C/300°F/Gas 2. Make a thick layer of half the potato slices in the base of a large, heavy, flameproof casserole, then cover with half the onion. Sprinkle with half the thyme and season with salt and pepper.

2 Heat the butter and oil in a large frying pan over medium heat. Add the bacon and chicken and cook, turning frequently, for 8–10 minutes, until the chicken is browned all over. Using a slotted spoon transfer the chicken and bacon to the casserole. Reserve the fat in the pan. Sprinkle the remaining thyme over the chicken and season with salt and pepper. Cover with the remaining onion, followed by a neat layer of overlapping potato slices. Season again with salt and pepper.

3 Pour the stock into the casserole, brush the potatoes with the reserved fat, then cover with a tight-fitting lid and cook in the oven for about 2 hours, until the chicken is tender.

4 Meanwhile, preheat the grill (broiler). Lift the casserole from the oven and remove the lid. Place under the grill and cook until the slices of potatoes are beginning to turn golden brown and crisp. Serve immediately.

Variation

Instead of using large chicken portions, use thighs or drumsticks, or a mixture of the two.

Chicken with Red Cabbage

Crushed juniper berries provide a distinctive flavour in this unusual casserole.

Serves 4

50g/2oz/¼ cup butter
4 large chicken portions, halved
1 onion, chopped

500g/1¼lb/5 cups finely
*   shredded red cabbage*
4 juniper berries, crushed
12 cooked chestnuts
120ml/4fl oz/½ cup full-bodied
*   red wine*
salt and ground black pepper

1 Melt the butter in a heavy, flameproof casserole over medium-low heat. Add the chicken pieces and cook, turning frequently, for 8–10 minutes, until lightly browned all over. Transfer the chicken to a plate using tongs.

2 Add the onion to the casserole and cook, stirring occasionally, for about 10 minutes, until softened and light golden brown. Stir the cabbage and juniper berries into the casserole, season with salt and pepper and cook over medium heat, stirring once or twice, for 6–7 minutes.

3 Stir the chestnuts into the casserole, then tuck the chicken pieces under the cabbage so that they are on the base of the casserole. Pour in the red wine.

4 Cover and cook gently for about 40 minutes, until the chicken juices run clear when the thickest part is pierced with the tip of a sharp knife and the cabbage is very tender. Taste and adjust the seasoning, if necessary, and serve immediately.

Cook's Tip

Red cabbage needs to be braised gently to be sure that it will be tender. Cooking it in red wine is a traditional accompaniment to game, but it works extremely well with chicken. The red wine helps to maintain the spectacular colour and you could also use ruby port for a slightly richer flavour. Juniper berries add a delightful resinous aroma to the dish.

Stoved Chicken Energy 524kcal/2206kJ; Protein 50.9g; Carbohydrate 48.2g, of which sugars 8.9g; Fat 15.5g, of which saturates 6g; Cholesterol 185mg; Calcium 53mg; Fibre 3.9g; Sodium 496mg.
With Red Cabbage Energy 405kcal/1697kJ; Protein 44.9g; Carbohydrate 18.6g, of which sugars 9.2g; Fat 14.9g, of which saturates 7.7g; Cholesterol 189mg; Calcium 94mg; Fibre 4.1g; Sodium 229mg.

Chicken Parcels with Herb Butter

These delightful individual filo pastry parcels contain a wonderfully moist and herb-flavoured filling.

Serves 4
4 skinless chicken breast fillets (about 175g/6oz each)
150g/5oz/generous ½ cup butter, softened, plus extra for greasing
90ml/6 tbsp mixed chopped fresh herbs, such as thyme, parsley, oregano and rosemary
5ml/1 tsp lemon juice
5 large sheets filo pastry, thawed if frozen
1 egg, beaten
30ml/2 tbsp freshly grated Parmesan cheese
salt and ground black pepper

1 Season the chicken fillets on both sides with salt and pepper. Melt 25g/1oz/2 tbsp of the butter in a frying pan over medium heat. Add the chicken and cook, turning once, for about 5 minutes, until lightly browned on both sides. Remove from the pan and leave to cool.

2 Preheat the oven to 190°C/375°F/Gas 5. Lightly grease a baking sheet with butter. Put the remaining measured butter, the herbs and lemon juice in a food processor or blender, season with salt and pepper and process until smooth. Melt half of this herb butter.

3 Take one sheet of filo pastry and brush with melted herb butter. Keep the other sheets covered with a damp dish towel. Fold the filo pastry sheet in half and brush again with butter. Place a chicken portion about 2.5cm/1in from the top end.

4 Dot the chicken with a quarter of the unmelted herb butter. Fold in the sides of the dough, then roll up to enclose the chicken completely. Place seam-side down on a lightly greased baking sheet. Repeat with the other chicken portions.

5 Brush the filo parcels with beaten egg. Cut the last sheet of filo into strips, then scrunch and arrange on top. Brush the parcels with the egg glaze, then sprinkle with Parmesan cheese. Bake for 35–50 minutes, until golden brown. Serve hot.

Turkey Hot-pot

Turkey and sausages combine well with kidney beans and other vegetables in this hearty stew.

Serves 4
115g/4oz/scant ½ cup kidney beans, soaked overnight, drained and rinsed
40g/1½oz/3 tbsp butter
2 herb-flavoured pork sausages
450g/1lb turkey casserole meat
3 leeks, sliced
2 carrots, finely chopped
4 tomatoes, chopped
10–15ml/2–3 tsp tomato purée (paste)
1 bouquet garni
400ml/14fl oz/1½ cups chicken stock
salt and ground black pepper

1 Put the kidney beans in a pan, add water to cover and bring to the boil. Boil vigorously for 15 minutes, then drain and return to the pan. Add water to cover, bring to the boil, lower the heat and simmer for 40 minutes. Drain well and set aside.

2 Meanwhile, melt the butter in a flameproof casserole over medium-low heat. Add the sausages and cook, turning frequently, for 7–8 minutes, until browned all over and the fat runs. Remove from the casserole with tongs and drain well on kitchen paper.

3 Stir the turkey into the casserole and cook, stirring occasionally, for about 5 minutes, until lightly browned all over, then transfer to a bowl using a slotted spoon.

4 Stir the leeks and carrot into the casserole and cook, stirring occasionally, for about 8 minutes, until lightly browned. Add the chopped tomatoes and tomato purée and simmer gently for about 5 minutes.

5 Chop the sausages and return to the casserole with the beans, turkey, bouquet garni and stock and season to taste with salt and pepper. Lower the heat, cover with a tight-fitting lid and simmer gently for about 1¼ hours, until the beans are tender and there is very little liquid. Spoon the stew on to warmed serving plates and serve immediately.

Chicken Energy 554kcal/2310kJ; Protein 42.5g; Carbohydrate 14.8g, of which sugars 0.5g; Fat 36.6g, of which saturates 22g; Cholesterol 240mg; Calcium 138mg; Fibre 0.6g; Sodium 417mg.
Turkey Energy 474kcal/1994kJ; Protein 51.9g; Carbohydrate 27.9g, of which sugars 13.1g; Fat 18g, of which saturates 9g; Cholesterol 115mg; Calcium 116mg; Fibre 11.8g; Sodium 308mg.

Duck with Cumberland Sauce

A sophisticated dish: the sauce contains both port and brandy, making it very rich and quite delicious.

Serves 4
4 duck portions
grated rind and juice of 1 lemon
grated rind and juice of
  1 large orange
60ml/4 tbsp redcurrant jelly
60ml/4 tbsp port
pinch of ground mace or ginger
15ml/1 tbsp brandy
salt and ground black pepper
orange slices, to garnish

1 Preheat the oven to 190°C/375°F/Gas 5. Place a rack in a roasting pan. Prick the skin of the duck portions all over and sprinkle with salt and pepper. Place on the rack and roast for 45–50 minutes, until the skin is crisp and the juices run clear when the thickest part is pierced with the point of a knife.

2 Meanwhile, simmer the lemon and orange rinds and juices together in a small pan for 5 minutes.

3 Add the redcurrant jelly and stir until melted, then stir in the port. Bring to the boil and add the mace or ginger and salt and pepper, to taste.

4 Transfer the duck to a serving platter and keep warm. Pour the fat from the roasting pan, leaving the cooking juices. Place the pan over low heat and stir in the brandy. Cook, scraping the sediment from the base of the pan, and bring to the boil. Stir in the port mixture and serve with the duck, garnished with orange slices.

> **Cook's Tip**
> *Duck is well known for being a fatty bird. Pricking the skin helps to release the fat during cooking. A clean darning needle is ideal for this. You can also use a fork, but try not to pierce the flesh. If the duck is then roasted on a rack over a roasting pan, the fat will collect beneath the duck preventing it from sitting in a lake of grease.*

Spatchcocked Devilled Poussin

"Spatchcock" – also known as "butterflied" – refers to birds that have been split and skewered flat. This shortens the cooking time considerably.

Serves 4
15ml/1 tbsp English (hot) mustard
  powder
15ml/1 tbsp paprika
15ml/1 tbsp ground cumin
20ml/4 tsp tomato ketchup
15ml/1 tbsp lemon juice
65g/2½oz/5 tbsp butter, melted
4 poussins (about 450g/1lb each)
salt

1 Mix together the mustard, paprika, cumin, ketchup, lemon juice and a pinch of salt in a bowl until smooth, then gradually stir in the butter.

2 Using game shears or strong kitchen scissors, split each poussin along one side of the backbone, then cut down the other side of the backbone and remove it.

3 Open out a poussin, skin-side uppermost, then press down firmly with the heel of your hand. Pass a long skewer through one leg and out through the other to secure the bird open and flat. Repeat with the remaining birds.

4 Spread the mustard mixture evenly over the skin of the birds. Cover loosely and leave in a cool place for at least 2 hours to marinate. Preheat the grill (broiler).

5 Place the birds, skin-side uppermost, under the grill and cook for about 12 minutes. Turn the birds over, baste with any juices in the grill (broiler) pan, and cook for a further 7 minutes, until the juices run clear when the thickest part is pierced with the point of a knife. Serve immediately.

> **Cook's Tip**
> *For an al fresco meal in the summer, these spatchcocked poussins may be cooked on a barbecue.*

Duck Energy 277kcal/1162kJ; Protein 29.7g; Carbohydrate 12.2g, of which sugars 12.2g; Fat 9.8g, of which saturates 3g; Cholesterol 165mg; Calcium 21mg; Fibre 0g; Sodium 170mg.
Poussin Energy 659kcal/2742kJ; Protein 50.2g; Carbohydrate 3g, of which sugars 2.9g; Fat 49.8g, of which saturates 18.4g; Cholesterol 296mg; Calcium 22mg; Fibre 0.1g; Sodium 442mg.

Poussins with Grapes in Vermouth

This sauce could also be served with roast chicken, but poussins have the stronger flavour.

Serves 4

4 poussins (about 450g/1lb each)
50g/2oz/¼ cup butter, softened
2 shallots, chopped
60ml/4 tbsp chopped
   fresh parsley
225g/8oz/2 cups white grapes,
   preferably Muscatel, halved
   and seeded

150ml/¼ pint/⅔ cup white
   vermouth
5ml/1 tsp cornflour (cornstarch)
60ml/4 tbsp double
   (heavy) cream
30ml/2 tbsp pine
   nuts, toasted
salt and ground black pepper
watercress sprigs or mizuna,
   to garnish

1 Preheat the oven to 200°C/400°F/Gas 6. Spread the softened butter all over the poussins and put a hazelnut-sized piece in the cavity of each bird.

2 Mix together the shallots and parsley and place a quarter of the mixture inside each poussin. Put the poussins side by side in a large roasting pan and roast for 40–50 minutes, or until the juices run clear when the thickest part is pierced with the point of a sharp knife. Transfer the poussins to a warmed serving plate. Cover and keep warm.

3 Skim off most of the fat from the roasting pan, then add the grapes and vermouth. Place the pan over a low heat for a few minutes to warm and slightly soften the grapes. Lift the grapes out of the pan using a slotted spoon and place them around the poussins. Keep covered.

4 Stir the cornflour into the cream until smooth, then add to the pan juices. Cook gently, stirring constantly, for 3–4 minutes, until the sauce has thickened slightly. Season to taste with salt and pepper. Spoon the sauce around the poussins. Sprinkle with the toasted pine nuts and garnish with watercress sprigs or mizuna. Serve immediately.

Rabbit with Mustard

Farmed rabbit is now becoming increasingly available in larger supermarkets, ready prepared and cut into serving portions.

Serves 4

15g/½oz/2 tbsp plain (all-
   purpose) flour
15ml/1 tbsp English (hot)
   mustard powder
4 large rabbit portions
25g/1oz/2 tbsp butter
30ml/2 tbsp sunflower oil
1 onion, finely chopped

150ml/¼ pint/⅔ cup beer
300ml/½ pint/1¼ cups chicken
   or veal stock
15ml/1 tbsp tarragon vinegar
25g/1oz/2 tbsp dark brown sugar
10–15ml/2–3 tsp prepared
   English mustard
salt and ground black pepper

To finish

50g/2oz/4 tbsp butter
30ml/2 tbsp sunflower oil
50g/2oz/1 cup fresh breadcrumbs
15ml/1 tbsp chopped fresh chives
15ml/1 tbsp chopped
   fresh tarragon

1 Preheat the oven to 160°C/325°F/Gas 3. Mix the flour and mustard powder together on a plate. Dip the rabbit portions in the flour mixture to coat. Reserve the excess flour.

2 Heat the butter and oil in a heavy, flameproof casserole over medium heat. Add the rabbit and cook, turning frequently, for 8–10 minutes, until browned all over. Transfer to a plate.

3 Lower the heat, add the onion to the pan and cook, stirring occasionally, for 5 minutes, until softened. Stir in any reserved flour mixture and cook, stirring, for 1 minute, then stir in the beer, stock and vinegar. Bring to the boil and add the sugar and black pepper. Simmer for 2 minutes. Return the rabbit and any juices that have collected to the casserole, cover with a tight-fitting lid and cook in the oven for 1 hour. Stir in the mustard and salt to taste, cover again and cook for a further 15 minutes.

4 To finish, heat together the butter and oil in a frying pan and fry the breadcrumbs, stirring frequently, until golden, then stir in the herbs. Transfer the rabbit to a warmed serving dish and sprinkle the breadcrumb mixture over the top.

Poussins Energy 831kcal/3456kJ; Protein 52.1g; Carbohydrate 12.3g, of which sugars 11.1g; Fat 60.2g, of which saturates 21.8g; Cholesterol 308mg; Calcium 62mg; Fibre 1.2g; Sodium 270mg.
Rabbit Energy 531kcal/2209kJ; Protein 31.8g; Carbohydrate 21.3g, of which sugars 8.7g; Fat 35g, of which saturates 14.6g; Cholesterol 187mg; Calcium 48mg; Fibre 0.6g; Sodium 247mg.

Pot-roast of Venison

The venison is marinated for 24 hours before preparation to give this rich dish an even fuller flavour.

Serves 4–5

1.75kg/4lb boned leg or shoulder of venison
75ml/5 tbsp sunflower oil
4 cloves
8 black peppercorns, lightly crushed
12 juniper berries, lightly crushed
250ml/8fl oz/1 cup full-bodied red wine
115g/4oz lightly smoked streaky (fatty) bacon, chopped
2 onions, finely chopped
2 carrots, chopped
150g/5oz large mushrooms, sliced
15g/½ oz/2 tbsp plain (all-purpose) flour
250ml/8fl oz/1 cup veal stock
30ml/2 tbsp redcurrant jelly
salt and ground black pepper

1 Put the venison in a bowl, add half the oil, the cloves, peppercorns, juniper berries and wine, cover with clear film (plastic wrap) and leave in a cold place or the refrigerator for 24 hours, turning the meat occasionally.

2 Preheat the oven to 160°C/325°F/Gas 3. Remove the venison from the bowl and pat dry. Reserve the marinade. Heat the remaining oil in a large shallow pan over medium heat. Add the venison and cook, turning once, for about 10 minutes, until evenly browned on both sides. Transfer to a plate.

3 Stir the bacon, onions, carrots and mushrooms into the pan and cook, stirring occasionally, for about 5 minutes. Stir in the flour and cook, stirring constantly, for 2 minutes, then remove the pan from the heat and gradually stir in the reserved marinade, stock and redcurrant jelly. Season with salt and pepper. Return the pan to the heat and bring to the boil, stirring constantly. Lower the heat and simmer for 2–3 minutes.

4 Transfer the venison and sauce to a casserole and cover with a tight-fitting lid. Cook in the oven, turning the the venison occasionally, for about 3 hours, until very tender. Remove the venison from the casserole and divide the sauce among warmed plates. Carve the venison and place on top. Serve.

Pheasant with Mushrooms

The wine and mushroom sauce in this recipe is given a lift by the inclusion of anchovy fillets.

Serves 4

1 pheasant, cut into portions
250ml/8fl oz/1 cup red wine
45ml/3 tbsp sunflower oil
60ml/4 tbsp Spanish sherry vinegar
1 large onion, chopped
2 rashers (strips) smoked bacon
350g/12oz chestnut (cremini) mushrooms, sliced
3 canned anchovy fillets, drained, soaked in water for 10 minutes and drained
350ml/12fl oz/1½ cups game, veal or chicken stock
1 bouquet garni
salt and ground black pepper

1 Place the pheasant portions in a dish. Add the wine, half the oil and half the vinegar, then sprinkle with half the onion. Season with salt and pepper. Cover the dish with clear film (plastic wrap) and leave in a cold place or the refrigerator, turning the pheasant portions occasionally, for 8–12 hours.

2 Preheat the oven to 160°C/325°F/Gas 3. Lift the pheasant portions from the dish and pat dry with kitchen paper. Reserve the marinade.

3 Heat the remaining oil in a flameproof casserole over medium heat. Add the pheasant portions and cook, turning frequently, for 8–10 minutes, until evenly browned all over. Transfer to a plate.

4 Cut the bacon into strips, then add to the casserole with the remaining onion. Cook over low heat, stirring occasionally, for 5 minutes, until the onion is softened but not coloured. Stir in the mushrooms and cook for about 3 minutes.

5 Stir in the anchovies and remaining vinegar and boil until reduced. Add the marinade, cook for 2 minutes, then add the stock and bouquet garni. Return the pheasant to the casserole, cover and bake for about 1½ hours. Transfer the pheasant to a serving dish. Boil the juices to reduce. Discard the bouquet garni, pour the juices over the pheasant and serve immediately.

Venison Energy 601kcal/2528kJ; Protein 83.1g; Carbohydrate 13g, of which sugars 9.6g; Fat 22.9g, of which saturates 5.9g; Cholesterol 187mg; Calcium 49mg; Fibre 1.9g; Sodium 566mg.
Pheasant Energy 457kcal/1910kJ; Protein 46.2g; Carbohydrate 6.4g, of which sugars 4.5g; Fat 23.1g, of which saturates 6.1g; Cholesterol 9mg; Calcium 102mg; Fibre 2g; Sodium 483mg.

Chicken, Leek & Parsley Pie

A filling pie with a two-cheese sauce, this dish is ideal for serving on a cold winter's day.

Serves 4–6

3 skinless chicken breast fillets
1 carrot, thickly sliced
1 small onion, quartered
6 black peppercorns
1 bouquet garni
450g/1lb shortcrust pastry dough, thawed if frozen
50g/2oz/1/4 cup butter
2 leeks, thinly sliced

50g/2oz/1/4 cup grated
   Cheddar cheese
25g/1oz/1/3 cup freshly grated
   Parmesan cheese
45ml/3 tbsp chopped
   fresh parsley
30ml/2 tbsp wholegrain mustard
5ml/1 tsp cornflour (cornstarch)
300ml/1/2 pint/11/4 cups double
   (heavy) cream
beaten egg, to glaze
salt and ground black pepper
mixed green salad leaves, to serve

1 Put the chicken, carrot, onion, peppercorns and bouquet garni in a shallow pan, add water and bring just to the boil. Lower the heat and poach gently, for 20–30 minutes, until tender. Leave to cool in the liquid, then drain and cut into strips.

2 Preheat the oven to 200°C/400°F/Gas 6. Divide the dough into two pieces, one slightly larger than the other. Use the larger piece to line an 18 x 28cm/7 x 11in baking tin (pan). Prick the base, bake for 15 minutes, then leave to cool.

3 Melt the butter in a frying pan over low heat. Add the leeks and cook, stirring occasionally, for 5–8 minutes, until soft. Stir in the cheeses and parsley.

4 Spread half the leek mixture over the pastry base, cover with the chicken strips, then top with the remaining leek mixture. Mix together the mustard, cornflour and cream in a bowl. Season with salt and pepper and pour into the pie.

5 Moisten the pastry base edges. Use the remaining pastry to cover the pie. Brush with beaten egg and bake for 30–40 minutes, until golden and crisp. Serve with salad.

Hampshire Farmhouse Flan

This English flan will satisfy even the heartiest appetite.

Serves 4

225g/8oz/2 cups wholemeal
   (whole-wheat) flour
50g/2oz/1/4 cup butter, cubed
50g/2oz/1/4 cup white cooking fat
5ml/1 tsp caraway seeds
5ml/1 tbsp vegetable oil
1 onion, chopped
1 garlic clove, crushed
225g/8oz/2 cups chopped
   cooked chicken

75g/3oz watercress or baby
   spinach leaves, chopped
grated rind of 1/2 lemon
2 eggs, lightly beaten
175ml/6fl oz/3/4 cup double
   (heavy) cream
45ml/3 tbsp natural (plain) yogurt
large pinch of grated nutmeg
45ml/3 tbsp grated
   Caerphilly cheese
beaten egg, to glaze
salt and ground black pepper

1 Put the flour into a bowl with a pinch of salt. Add the butter and cooking fat and rub in with your fingertips until the mixture resembles breadcrumbs.

2 Stir in the caraway seeds and 45ml/3 tbsp iced water and mix to a firm dough. Knead until smooth, then use to line an 18 x 28cm/7 x 11in loose-based flan tin (pan). Reserve the dough trimmings. Prick the base and chill for 20 minutes. Heat a baking sheet in the oven at 200°C/400°F/Gas 6.

3 Heat the oil in a frying pan over low heat. Add the onion and garlic and cook, stirring occasionally, for 5 minutes, until softened. Leave to cool. Meanwhile, line the pastry case (pie shell) with greaseproof (waxed) paper and baking beans. Bake for 10 minutes, remove the paper and beans and bake for a further 5 minutes.

4 Mix the onion mixture, chicken, watercress or spinach and lemon rind; spoon into the pastry case. Beat the eggs, cream, yogurt, nutmeg, cheese and seasoning; pour over the chicken mixture. Cut the pastry trimmings into 1cm/1/2in strips. Brush with egg, then twist and lay in a lattice over the flan. Press on the ends. Bake for 35 minutes, until golden.

Chicken Energy 620kcal/2584kJ; Protein 28.2g; Carbohydrate 39.4g, of which sugars 3.2g; Fat 39.7g, of which saturates 24.1g; Cholesterol 151mg; Calcium 237mg; Fibre 3.3g; Sodium 218mg.
Flan Energy 773kcal/3216kJ; Protein 28.2g; Carbohydrate 38g, of which sugars 2.9g; Fat 57.4g, of which saturates 30.2g; Cholesterol 244mg; Calcium 181mg; Fibre 5.6g; Sodium 247mg.

Chicken Charter Pie

A light pie with a fresh taste; it is versatile enough to use for light meals or informal dinners.

Serves 4

50g/2oz/¼ cup butter
4 chicken legs
I onion, finely chopped
150ml/¼ pint/⅔ cup milk
150ml/¼ pint/⅔ cup sour cream

4 spring onions (scallions), cut into quarters
20g/¾oz/⅓ cup fresh parsley leaves, finely chopped
225g/8oz puff pastry dough, thawed if frozen
120ml/4fl oz/½ cup double (heavy) cream
2 eggs, beaten, plus extra for glazing
salt and ground black pepper

I Melt the butter in a frying pan over medium heat. Add the chicken legs and cook, turning frequently, for 8–10 minutes, until evenly browned all over. Transfer to a plate.

2 Add the onion to the pan, lower the heat and cook, stirring occasionally, for 5 minutes, until softened but not coloured. Stir the milk, sour cream, spring onions and parsley into the pan, season with salt and pepper and bring to the boil, then simmer for 2 minutes.

3 Return the chicken to the pan with any juices, cover and cook gently for 30 minutes. Transfer the chicken mixture to a 1.2 litre/2 pint/5 cup pie dish. Leave to cool.

4 Preheat the oven to 220°C/425°F/Gas 7. Place a narrow strip of pastry on the edge of the pie dish. Moisten the strip, then cover the dish with the pastry. Press the edges together. Make a hole in the centre of the pastry and insert a small funnel of foil. Brush the pastry with beaten egg to glaze, then bake for 15–20 minutes.

5 Lower the oven temperature to 180°C/350°F/Gas 4. Mix the cream and eggs, then pour into the pie through the funnel. Shake the pie to distribute the cream, then return to the oven for 5–10 minutes. Leave the pie in a warm place for about 5–10 minutes before serving, or cool completely.

Chicken & Ham Pie

This is a rich pie flavoured with fresh herbs and lightly spiced with mace – ideal for taking on a picnic.

Serves 8

400g/14oz shortcrust pastry dough, thawed if frozen
800g/1¾lb chicken breast portions
350g/12oz uncooked gammon (smoked or cured ham)

60ml/4 tbsp double (heavy) cream
6 spring onions (scallions), finely chopped
15ml/1 tbsp chopped fresh tarragon
10ml/2 tsp chopped fresh thyme
grated rind and juice of ½ large lemon
5ml/1 tsp ground mace
beaten egg or milk, to glaze
salt and ground black pepper

I Preheat the oven to 190°C/375°F/Gas 5. Roll out one-third of the pastry dough and use it to line a 20cm/8in pie tin (pan), 5cm/2in deep. Place on a baking sheet.

2 Mince (grind) 115g/4oz of the chicken with the gammon, then mix with the cream, spring onions, herbs, lemon rind and 15ml/1 tbsp of the lemon juice in a bowl. Season lightly with salt and pepper. Cut the remaining chicken into 1cm/½in pieces and mix with the remaining lemon juice and the mace in another bowl and season with salt and pepper.

3 Make a layer of one-third of the gammon mixture in the pastry base, cover with half the chopped chicken, then add another layer of one-third of the gammon. Add all the remaining chicken followed by the remaining gammon.

4 Dampen the edges of the pastry base and roll out the remaining pastry to make a lid for the pie. Use the trimmings to make a lattice decoration. Make a small hole in the centre of the pie, then brush the top with beaten egg or milk.

5 Bake the pie for 20 minutes. Lower the oven temperature to 160°C/325°F/Gas 3 and bake for a further 1–1¼ hours, until the pastry is golden brown. Transfer the pie to a wire rack and leave to cool before serving.

Charter Pie Energy 713kcal/2967kJ; Protein 37.8g; Carbohydrate 25g, of which sugars 4.9g; Fat 52.6g, of which saturates 22.8g; Cholesterol 250mg; Calcium 154mg; Fibre 0.4g; Sodium 426mg.
Chicken & Ham Pie Energy 431kcal/1803kJ; Protein 34.8g; Carbohydrate 23.8g, of which sugars 0.8g; Fat 22.5g, of which saturates 8.3g; Cholesterol 98mg; Calcium 57mg; Fibre 1.1g; Sodium 647mg.

Turkey Spirals

These little spirals may look difficult, but they're easy to make, and a very good way to pep up plain turkey.

Serves 4

4 thinly sliced turkey breast steaks
    (about 90g/3½oz each)
20ml/4 tsp tomato purée (paste)
15g/½oz/¼ cup large fresh
    basil leaves
1 garlic clove, crushed
15ml/1 tbsp skimmed milk
25g/1oz/2 tbsp wholemeal
    (whole-wheat) flour
salt and ground black pepper
passata (bottled strained
    tomatoes) or fresh tomato
    sauce, pasta and fresh basil,
    to serve

1 Preheat the grill (broiler). Place the turkey steaks on a board. Cover with clear film (plastic wrap) and flatten them slightly by beating gently with the side of a rolling pin.

2 Spread each turkey breast steak with tomato purée, then top with a few leaves of basil and a little crushed garlic. Season with salt and pepper.

3 Roll up firmly around the filling and secure with a wooden cocktail stick (toothpick). Brush with milk and sprinkle with flour to coat lightly.

4 Place the turkey rolls on a foil-lined grill (broiler) pan. Cook under a moderately hot grill, turning them occasionally, for 15–20 minutes, until thoroughly cooked.

5 Transfer the rolls to a chopping board and cut them into slices. Place the slices on warmed plates and serve with a spoonful or two of passata or fresh tomato sauce and pasta, sprinkled with fresh basil.

Variation
This recipe is also suitable for pork and veal escalopes (US scallops) and chicken breast portions.

Turkey & Mangetout Stir-fry

Have all the ingredients prepared before you start cooking this dish, as it will be ready in minutes.

Serves 4

30ml/2 tbsp sesame oil
90ml/6 tbsp lemon juice
1 garlic clove, crushed
1cm/½in piece fresh root ginger,
    peeled and grated
5ml/1 tsp clear honey
450g/1lb turkey fillets, cut
    into strips
115g/4oz/1 cup mangetouts
    (snow peas), trimmed
30ml/2 tbsp groundnut
    (peanut) oil
50g/2oz/½ cup cashew nuts
6 spring onions (scallions), cut
    into strips
225g/8oz can water chestnuts,
    drained and thinly sliced
pinch of salt
saffron rice, to serve

1 Mix together the sesame oil, lemon juice, garlic, ginger and honey in a shallow non-metallic dish. Add the turkey and mix well. Cover and leave to marinate for 3–4 hours.

2 Blanch the mangetouts in boiling salted water for about 1 minute. Drain and refresh under cold running water.

3 Drain the turkey strips and reserve the marinade. Heat the groundnut oil in a wok or large frying pan, add the cashews and stir-fry for 1–2 minutes, until golden brown. Remove the nuts from the pan using a slotted spoon and set aside.

4 Add the turkey and stir-fry for 3–4 minutes, until golden brown. Add the spring onions, mangetouts, water chestnuts and reserved marinade. Cook for a few minutes, until the turkey is tender and the sauce is bubbling and hot. Stir in the cashew nuts and serve immediately with saffron rice.

Cook's Tip
This dish could be served on a bed of medium-width egg noodles for a quick meal.

Spirals Energy 164kcal/696kJ; Protein 32.7g; Carbohydrate 4.9g, of which sugars 1g; Fat 1.7g, of which saturates 0.6g; Cholesterol 67mg; Calcium 13mg; Fibre 0.7g; Sodium 95mg.
Stir-fry Energy 369kcal/1546kJ; Protein 43.6g; Carbohydrate 5.3g, of which sugars 3.4g; Fat 19.5g, of which saturates 3.8g; Cholesterol 83mg; Calcium 52mg; Fibre 1.9g; Sodium 173mg.

Venison with Cranberry Sauce

Venison steaks are now readily available. Lean and low in fat, they make a healthy and delicious choice for a special occasion.

Serves 4

1 orange
1 lemon
75g/3oz/¾ cup fresh or frozen
   unthawed cranberries
5ml/1 tsp grated fresh root ginger
1 fresh thyme sprig, plus extra to
   garnish
5ml/1 tsp Dijon mustard
60ml/4 tbsp redcurrant jelly
150ml/¼ pint/⅔ cup port
30ml/2 tbsp sunflower oil
4 venison steaks
2 shallots, finely chopped
salt and ground black pepper
fresh thyme sprigs, to garnish
mashed potatoes and steamed
   broccoli, to serve

1 Pare the rind from half the orange and half the lemon using a vegetable peeler, then cut into very fine strips. Blanch the strips in a small pan of boiling water for 5 minutes, until tender. Drain the strips and refresh under cold water.

2 Squeeze the juice from the orange and lemon and pour into a small pan. Add the cranberries, ginger, thyme sprig, mustard, redcurrant jelly and port. Cook over medium-low heat, stirring frequently, until the jelly has melted. Bring to the boil, stirring constantly, cover and lower the heat. Simmer gently for 15 minutes, until the cranberries are just tender.

3 Heat the oil in a large, heavy frying pan over a high heat. Add the venison steaks and cook for 2–3 minutes. Turn them over and add the shallots. Cook on the other side for 2–3 minutes, or until done to your taste. Just before the end of cooking, pour in the sauce and add the strips of orange and lemon rind. Leave the sauce to bubble for a few seconds to thicken slightly, then remove and discard the thyme sprig. Taste and adjust the seasoning, if necessary.

4 Transfer the venison steaks to warmed plates and spoon the sauce over them. Garnish with thyme sprigs and serve immediately accompanied by creamy mashed potatoes and steamed broccoli.

Farmhouse Venison Pie

A simple and satisfying pie; the venison is cooked in a rich gravy, topped with potato and parsnip mash.

Serves 4

45ml/3 tbsp sunflower oil
1 onion, chopped
1 garlic clove, crushed
3 rashers (strips) rindless streaky
   (fatty) bacon, chopped
675g/1½lb minced
   (ground) venison
115g/4oz button (white)
   mushrooms, chopped
25g/1oz/¼ cup plain (all-
   purpose) flour
450ml/¾ pint/scant 2 cups beef
   stock
150ml/¼ pint/⅔ cup port
2 bay leaves
5ml/1 tsp chopped fresh thyme
5ml/1 tsp Dijon mustard
15ml/1 tbsp redcurrant jelly
675g/1½lb potatoes
450g/1lb parsnips
1 egg yolk
50g/2oz/¼ cup butter
pinch of freshly grated nutmeg
45ml/3 tbsp chopped
   fresh parsley
salt and ground black pepper
green vegetables, to
   serve (optional)

1 Heat the oil in a large frying pan over low heat. Add the onion, garlic and bacon and cook, stirring occasionally, for about 5 minutes, until the onion is softened. Add the venison and mushrooms and cook for a few minutes, stirring, until browned.

2 Stir in the flour and cook for 1–2 minutes, then add the stock, port, herbs, mustard and redcurrant jelly. Season with salt and pepper. Bring to the boil, cover with a tight-fitting lid and simmer for 30–40 minutes, until tender. Spoon into a large pie dish or four individual ovenproof dishes.

3 While the venison and mushroom mixture is cooking, preheat the oven to 200°C/400°F/Gas 6. Cut the potatoes and parsnips into large chunks. Cook together in salted boiling water for 20 minutes, or until tender. Drain and mash, then beat in the egg yolk, butter, nutmeg, parsley and seasoning.

4 Spread the potato and parsnip mixture over the meat and bake for 30–40 minutes, until hot and golden brown. Serve immediately with green vegetables, if you like.

Venison Energy 259kcal/1092kJ; Protein 33.7g; Carbohydrate 14.1g, of which sugars 13.5g; Fat 8.9g, of which saturates 1.9g; Cholesterol 75mg; Calcium 16mg; Fibre 0.7g; Sodium 91mg.
Farmhouse Pie Energy 723kcal/3033kJ; Protein 48.5g; Carbohydrate 59.6g, of which sugars 20.4g; Fat 30.3g, of which saturates 11.2g; Cholesterol 174mg; Calcium 128mg; Fibre 9g; Sodium 447mg.

Lamb Pie with Mustard Thatch

This makes a pleasant change from a classic shepherd's pie – and it is a healthier option, as well.

Serve 4
750g/1½lb potatoes, diced
30ml/2 tbsp skimmed milk
15ml/1 tbsp wholegrain or
  French mustard
450g/1lb lean minced
  (ground) lamb

1 onion, chopped
2 celery sticks, sliced
2 carrots, diced
150ml/¼ pint/⅔ cup beef stock
60ml/4 tbsp rolled oats
15ml/1 tbsp Worcestershire sauce
30ml/2 tbsp chopped fresh
  rosemary or 10ml/2 tsp
  dried rosemary
salt and ground black pepper
fresh vegetables, to serve

1 Cook the potatoes in boiling lightly salted water for about 20 minutes, until tender. Drain well and mash until smooth, then stir in the milk and mustard. Meanwhile, preheat the oven to 200°C/400°F/Gas 6.

2 Break up the lamb with a fork and cook without any additional fat in a non-stick pan until lightly browned. Add the onion, celery and carrots to the pan and cook for 2–3 minutes, stirring constantly.

3 Stir in the stock and rolled oats. Bring to the boil, then add the Worcestershire sauce and rosemary and season to taste with salt and pepper.

4 Turn the meat mixture into a 1.75 litre/3 pint/7½ cup ovenproof dish and spread the potato topping evenly over the top, swirling with the edge of a knife. Bake for 30–35 minutes, or until golden. Serve hot with fresh vegetables.

> **Variation**
> Substitute low-fat natural (plain) yogurt for the milk and 30ml/2 tbsp chopped fresh mint for the mustard for a herb-flavoured thatch that is still a healthy option.

Lancashire Hot-pot

Browning the lamb and kidneys, plus the extra vegetables and herbs, adds flavour to the traditional basic ingredients.

Serves 4
45ml/3 tbsp vegetable oil
8 medium neck (US shoulder)
  lamb chops (about 900g/2lb
  total weight)
175g/6oz lamb's kidneys, cored
  and cut into large pieces

900g/2lb potatoes, thinly sliced
3 carrots, thickly sliced
450g/1lb leeks, sliced
3 celery sticks, sliced
15ml/1 tbsp chopped fresh thyme
30ml/2 tbsp chopped
  fresh parsley
small fresh rosemary sprig
600ml/1 pint/2½ cups veal or
  chicken stock
salt and ground black pepper

1 Preheat the oven to 170°C/325°F/Gas 3. Heat the oil in a frying pan over medium heat. Add the chops, in batches if necessary, and cook for 2–3 minutes on each side, until evenly browned. Transfer to a plate.

2 Add the kidneys to the pan, in batches if necessary, and cook for 1–2 minutes on each side, until evenly browned. Transfer to the plate with the chops. Reserve the fat in the pan.

3 Make alternate layers of lamb chops, kidneys, three-quarters of the potatoes and the carrots, leeks and celery. Sprinkle the herbs over each layer as you go and season each layer with salt and pepper. Tuck the rosemary sprig down the side.

4 Arrange the remaining potato slices on top to cover the meat and vegetables completely. Pour over the veal or chicken stock, brush the potato topping with the reserved fat from the frying pan, then cover the casserole with a tight-fitting lid and bake for 2½ hours.

5 Increase the oven temperature to 220°C/425°F/Gas 7. Uncover the casserole and cook for a further 30 minutes, until the potato topping is golden brown. Serve immediately straight from the casserole.

Hot-Pot Energy 810kcal/3400kJ; Protein 76.7g; Carbohydrate 43.7g, of which sugars 9.3g; Fat 37.8g, of which saturates 13.2g; Cholesterol 363mg; Calcium 140mg; Fibre 6.2g; Sodium 285mg.
Lamb Pie Energy 382kcal/1605kJ; Protein 25.9g; Carbohydrate 35.1g, of which sugars 6.8g; Fat 16.4g, of which saturates 7.6g; Cholesterol 89mg; Calcium 78mg; Fibre 2.9g; Sodium 169mg.

Oatmeal & Herb Rack of Lamb

Ask the butcher to remove the chine bone that runs along the eye of the meat – this will make carving easier.

Serves 6

2 best end necks (cross rib) of lamb (about 900kg/2lb each)
finely grated rind of 1 lemon
60ml/4 tbsp medium oatmeal
50g/2oz/1 cup fresh white breadcrumbs
60ml/4 tbsp chopped fresh parsley
25g/1oz/2 tbsp butter, melted
30ml/2 tbsp clear honey
salt and ground black pepper
fresh herb sprigs, to garnish
roasted baby vegetables and gravy, to serve

1 Preheat the oven to 200°C/400°F/Gas 6. Using a small sharp knife, cut through the skin and meat of both pieces of lamb about 2.5cm/1in from the tips of the bones. Pull off the fatty meat to expose the bones, then scrape around each bone tip until completely clean.

2 Trim all the skin and most of the fat from the meat, then lightly score the remaining fat with a sharp knife. Repeat with the second rack.

3 Mix together the lemon rind, oatmeal, breadcrumbs and parsley in a bowl. Season with salt and pepper and stir in the melted butter until thoroughly combined.

4 Brush the fatty side of each rack of lamb with honey, then press the oatmeal mixture evenly over the surface with your fingers until well coated.

5 Place the racks in a roasting pan with the oatmeal sides uppermost. Roast for 40–50 minutes, depending on whether you like rare or medium lamb. Cover loosely with foil if browning too much.

6 To serve, slice each rack into three and place two chops on each of six warmed plates. Garnish with fresh herb sprigs and serve immediately with roasted baby vegetables and gravy made with the pan juices.

Skewers of Lamb with Mint

For a more substantial meal, you could serve these skewers on a bed of flavoured rice or couscous.

Serves 4

300ml/½ pint/1¼ cups Greek (US strained plain) yogurt
½ garlic clove, crushed
generous pinch of saffron powder
30ml/2 tbsp chopped fresh mint
30ml/2 tbsp clear honey
45ml/3 tbsp olive oil
3 lamb neck (US shoulder) fillets (about 675g/1½ lb total)
1 aubergine (eggplant), cut into 2.5cm/1in cubes
2 small red onions, quartered
salt and ground black pepper
small fresh mint leaves, to garnish
mixed salad and hot pitta bread, to serve

1 Mix together the yogurt, garlic, saffron, mint, honey and oil in a shallow dish and season with pepper.

2 Trim the lamb and cut into 2.5cm/1in cubes. Add to the marinade and stir until well coated. Cover with clear film (plastic wrap) and leave to marinate in the refrigerator for at least 4 hours or preferably overnight.

3 Blanch the diced aubergine in a pan of salted boiling water for 1–2 minutes. Drain well and pat dry on kitchen paper.

4 Preheat the grill (broiler). Drain the lamb and reserve the marinade. Thread the lamb, aubergine and onion pieces alternately on to skewers. (If you are using wooden skewers, soak them in water for 30 minutes first to prevent them from charring during cooking.)

5 Grill (broil) for 10–12 minutes, turning and basting occasionally with the reserved marinade, until the lamb and vegetables are tender. Alternatively, cook the kebabs on the barbecue for the same length of time.

6 Transfer the skewers to plates and serve immediately, garnished with mint leaves and accompanied by a mixed salad and hot pitta bread.

Lamb Rack Energy 719kcal/2979kJ; Protein 40g; Carbohydrate 15g, of which sugars 1.4g; Fat 55.9g, of which saturates 27.1g; Cholesterol 171mg; Calcium 59mg; Fibre 1.2g; Sodium 227mg.
Skewers Energy 526kcal/2194kJ; Protein 39.7g; Carbohydrate 15.4g, of which sugars 13.4g; Fat 35.4g, of which saturates 14g; Cholesterol 128mg; Calcium 155mg; Fibre 3.1g; Sodium 204mg.

Lamb with Mint Sauce

In this flavoursome dish, the classic British combination of lamb and mint is given an original twist.

Serves 4
8 lamb noisettes, 2–2.5cm/
    ¾–1 in thick
30ml/2 tbsp vegetable oil
45ml/3 tbsp medium-bodied dry
    white wine, or vegetable or
    veal stock

salt and ground black pepper
fresh mint sprigs, to garnish

For the sauce
30ml/2 tbsp boiling water
5–10ml/1–2 tsp sugar
leaves from a small bunch of
    fresh mint, finely chopped
about 30ml/2 tbsp white
    wine vinegar

1 To make the sauce, stir the water and sugar together in a heatproof bowl, then add the mint and vinegar to taste. Season with salt and pepper. Leave to stand for 30 minutes.

2 Season the lamb with pepper. Heat the oil in a large, heavy frying pan. Add the lamb, in batches if necessary so that the pan is not crowded, and cook for about 3 minutes on each side for meat that is pink in the middle.

3 Transfer the lamb to a warmed plate and season with salt, then cover and keep warm.

4 Stir the wine or stock into the cooking juices, scraping up the sediment from the base of the pan, and bring to the boil. Leave to bubble for a couple of minutes, then pour over the lamb. Garnish the lamb noisettes with small sprigs of mint and serve hot with the mint sauce.

> **Cook's Tip**
> In the past, cooks used more sugar to counteract the sharpness of the vinegar in the mint sauce. Add more to taste, if you like. It was also common to sprinkle the mint leaves with 5ml/1 tsp sugar before chopping them finely.

Sausage & Bean Ragoût

This is an economical and nutritious main course that children will love. Serve with warm garlic and herb bread, if you like.

Serves 4
350g/12oz/2 cups dried flageolet
    or cannellini beans, soaked
    overnight in cold water
45ml/3 tbsp olive oil
1 onion, finely chopped
2 garlic cloves, crushed

450g/1lb good-quality chunky
    sausages, skinned and
    thickly sliced
15ml/1 tbsp tomato
    purée (paste)
400g/14oz can chopped
    tomatoes
30ml/2 tbsp chopped
    fresh parsley
15ml/1 tbsp chopped fresh thyme
salt and ground black pepper
chopped fresh thyme and parsley,
    to garnish

1 Drain and rinse the soaked beans and place them in a pan with enough water to cover. Bring to the boil, cover the pan with a tight-fitting lid and simmer for about 1 hour, or until tender. Drain the beans and set aside.

2 Heat the oil in a frying pan over medium-low heat. Add the onion, garlic and sausages and cook, stirring and turning occasionally, until golden.

3 Stir in the tomato purée, tomatoes, chopped parsley and thyme. Season with salt and pepper, then bring to the boil.

4 Add the beans, lower the heat, cover with a lid and cook gently, stirring occasionally, for about 15 minutes, until the sausage slices are cooked through. Divide the ragoût among warmed plates, garnish with chopped fresh thyme and parsley and serve immediately.

> **Cook's Tip**
> For a spicier version, add some skinned, thinly sliced chorizo or kabanos sausage along with the cooked beans for the last 15 minutes of cooking.

Lamb Energy 332kcal/1384kJ; Protein 29.6g; Carbohydrate 1.6g, of which sugars 1.4g; Fat 22.3g, of which saturates 8.5g; Cholesterol 114mg; Calcium 22mg; Fibre 0g; Sodium 130mg.
Ragoût Energy 745kcal/3114kJ; Protein 32.3g; Carbohydrate 54.1g, of which sugars 8.2g; Fat 45.9g, of which saturates 15.2g; Cholesterol 53mg; Calcium 146mg; Fibre 15.6g; Sodium 889mg.

Pork with Plums

Plums poached in apple juice are used here to make a delightfully fruity sauce for pork chops.

Serves 4

450g/1lb ripe plums, halved and stoned (pitted)
300ml/½ pint/1¼ cups apple juice
40g/1½oz/3 tbsp butter
15ml/1 tbsp oil
4 pork chops (about 200g/7oz each)
1 onion, finely chopped
pinch of freshly ground mace
salt and ground black pepper
fresh sage leaves, to garnish

1 Put the plums and the apple juice in a pan and bring just to the boil. Lower the heat and simmer until tender. Strain off and reserve the juice. Place half the plums and a little of the juice in a food processor or blender and process to a purée.

2 Meanwhile, heat the butter and oil in a large frying pan over medium heat. Add the chops and cook for about 4 minutes on each side until evenly browned. Transfer them to a plate.

3 Add the onion to the frying pan and lower the heat. Cook, stirring occasionally, for about 5 minutes, until it is softened but not coloured.

4 Return the chops to the pan. Pour over the plum purée and all the reserved apple juice. Simmer, uncovered, for 10–15 minutes, until the chops are cooked through.

5 Add the remaining plums to the pan, then add the mace and season to taste with salt and pepper. Warm the sauce through over medium heat and serve garnished with fresh sage leaves.

Cook's Tip
When buying plums, look for firm fruit with a little "give" but avoid any that are squashy. Use within one or two days of purchase because they over-ripen very rapidly.

Pork Loin with Celery

Have a change from a plain Sunday roast and try this whole loin of pork in an unusual celery and cream sauce instead.

Serves 4

15ml/1 tbsp vegetable oil
50g/2oz/¼ cup butter
1kg/2¼lb boned, rolled loin of pork, rind removed and trimmed
1 onion, chopped
1 bouquet garni
3 fresh dill sprigs
150ml/¼ pint/⅔ cup dry white wine
150ml/¼ pint/⅔ cup water
sticks from 1 celery head, cut into 2.5cm/1in lengths
25g/1oz/¼ cup plain (all-purpose) flour
150ml/¼ pint/⅔ cup double (heavy) cream
squeeze of lemon juice
salt and ground black pepper
chopped fresh dill, to garnish

1 Heat the oil and half the butter in a heavy flameproof casserole just large enough to hold the pork and celery. Add the pork and cook, turning frequently, for 8–10 minutes, until evenly browned. Transfer the pork to a plate.

2 Add the onion to the casserole, lower the heat and cook, stirring occasionally, for 5 minutes, until softened but not coloured. Add the bouquet garni and dill sprigs, place the pork on top and add any juices from the plate. Pour in the wine and water, season to taste, cover and simmer gently for 30 minutes.

3 Turn the pork, arrange the celery around it, cover again and cook for 40 minutes, until the pork and celery are tender. Transfer the pork and celery to a serving plate, cover and keep warm. Discard the bouquet garni and dill.

4 Cream the remaining butter with the flour, then whisk into the cooking liquid while it is barely simmering. Cook for 2–3 minutes, stirring occasionally. Stir the cream into the casserole, bring to the boil and add a squeeze of lemon juice.

5 Slice the pork, spoon a little sauce over the slices and garnish with dill. Serve with the remaining sauce handed separately.

Pork Energy 620kcal/2595kJ; Protein 65.4g; Carbohydrate 17.4g, of which sugars 17.4g; Fat 32.6g, of which saturates 13.1g; Cholesterol 241mg; Calcium 40mg; Fibre 1.8g; Sodium 232mg.
Pork Loin Energy 669kcal/2783kJ; Protein 55.6g; Carbohydrate 8.1g, of which sugars 3g; Fat 43.5g, of which saturates 22.9g; Cholesterol 236mg; Calcium 105mg; Fibre 1.8g; Sodium 336mg.

Somerset Pork with Apples

A creamy cider sauce accompanies tender pieces of pork and sliced apples to make a rich supper dish.

Serves 4
25g/1oz/2 tbsp butter
500g/1¼lb pork loin, cut into
    bitesize pieces
12 baby (pearl) onions, peeled
10ml/2 tsp grated lemon rind

300ml/½ pint/1¼ cups dry
    (hard) cider
150ml/¼ pint/⅔ cup veal stock
2 crisp eating apples such as
    Granny Smith, cored and sliced
45ml/3 tbsp chopped
    fresh parsley
100ml/3½fl oz/scant ½ cup
    whipping cream
salt and ground black pepper

1 Melt the butter in a large sauté or frying pan over medium heat. Add the pork, in batches, and cook, stirring frequently, for about 8 minutes, until browned all over. Transfer the pork to a bowl with a slotted spoon.

2 Add the onions to the pan and lower the heat. Cook, stirring occasionally, for 8–10 minutes, until lightly browned.

3 Stir in the lemon rind, cider and stock, bring to the boil and cook for about 3 minutes. Return all the pork to the pan, cover and simmer gently for about 25 minutes, until tender.

4 Add the apples to the pan and cook for a further 5 minutes. Using a slotted spoon, transfer the pork, onions and apples to a warmed serving dish, cover and keep warm.

5 Stir the parsley and cream into the pan and leave to bubble to thicken the sauce slightly. Season with salt and pepper, then pour over the pork and serve immediately.

> **Cook's Tip**
> *Veal stock is mellow in flavour and does not overpower other ingredients. The mainstay of restaurant kitchens, it's used less frequently at home. Chicken stock is a satisfactory alternative.*

Golden Pork & Apricot Casserole

The rich golden colour and warm spicy flavour of this simple casserole make it ideal for a chilly winter's day.

Serves 4
4 lean pork loin chops
1 onion, thinly sliced
2 yellow (bell) peppers, seeded
    and sliced

10ml/2 tsp medium curry powder
15g/½ oz/2 tbsp plain (all-
    purpose) flour
250ml/8fl oz/1 cup chicken stock
115g/4oz ready-to-eat
    dried apricots
30ml/2 tbsp wholegrain mustard
salt and ground black pepper
boiled rice or new potatoes, to
    serve (optional)

1 Trim the excess fat from the pork. Cook the chops, without any additional fat, in a large heavy or non-stick pan over medium heat for about 6 minutes, until lightly browned.

2 Lower the heat, add the onion and yellow peppers to the pan and cook, stirring frequently, for about 5 minutes, until softened but not coloured.

3 Stir in the curry powder and the flour and cook, stirring constantly, for 1 minute.

4 Gradually stir in the stock, then add the apricots and mustard and bring to the boil over medium heat. Cover with a tight-fitting lid, lower the heat and simmer gently for 25–30 minutes, until the chops are cooked through and tender. Season to taste with salt and pepper and serve immediately, with boiled rice or new potatoes, if you like.

> **Variations**
> *• This recipe also works well with chicken breast portions – with or without the skin – instead of pork chops. However, you will need to heat 15ml/1 tbsp sunflower oil in the pan for the initial browning in step 1.*
> *• Substitute the same quantity of ready-to-eat prunes for the apricots and use red (bell) peppers instead of yellow.*

Somerset Pork Energy 375kcal/1563kJ; Protein 28.7g; Carbohydrate 15g, of which sugars 12.7g; Fat 20.5g, of which saturates 11.3g; Cholesterol 118mg; Calcium 58mg; Fibre 2.2g; Sodium 141mg.
Golden Pork Energy 281kcal/1181kJ; Protein 34.9g; Carbohydrate 20.9g, of which sugars 16.7g; Fat 6.9g, of which saturates 2.2g; Cholesterol 95mg; Calcium 64mg; Fibre 4.1g; Sodium 124mg.

Stir-fried Pork with Mustard

Fry the apple for this dish very carefully, because it will disintegrate if it is overcooked.

Serves 4

500g/1¼lb pork fillet (tenderloin)
1 tart eating apple, such as
 Granny Smith
40g/1½oz/3 tbsp unsalted
 (sweet) butter
15g/½oz/1 tbsp caster
 (superfine) sugar
1 small onion, finely chopped
30ml/2 tbsp Calvados or brandy
15ml/1 tbsp Meaux or coarse
 grain mustard
15ml/¼ pint/⅔ cup double
 (heavy) cream
30ml/2 tbsp chopped
 fresh parsley
salt and ground black pepper
fresh flat leaf parsley sprigs,
 to garnish

1 Cut the pork fillet into thin even size slices with a sharp knife. Peel and core the apple, then cut it into thick slices.

2 Heat a wok, then add half the butter. When the butter is hot, add the apple slices, sprinkle the sugar over them and stir-fry for 2–3 minutes. Remove the apple from the wok and set aside. Wipe out the wok with kitchen paper.

3 Reheat the wok, then add the remaining butter and stir-fry the pork fillet and onion together for 2–3 minutes, until the pork is golden and the onion has begun to soften.

4 Stir in the Calvados or brandy, bring to the boil and cook until it has reduced by about half. Stir in the mustard.

5 Add the cream and simmer gently for about 1 minute, then stir in the parsley. Transfer to warmed plates, divide the apple among them and serve garnished with sprigs of flat leaf parsley.

> **Cook's Tip**
> If you haven't got a wok, use a large frying pan, preferably with deep, sloping sides.

Roast Pork with Sage & Onion

Pork roasted with a sage and onion stuffing makes a perfect Sunday lunch dish.

Serves 6–8

1.3–1.6kg/3–3½lb boneless loin
 of pork
60ml/4 tbsp fine, dry breadcrumbs
10ml/2 tsp chopped fresh sage
25ml/1½ tbsp plain (all-purpose)
 flour
300ml/½ pint/1¼ cups cider
150ml/¼ pint/⅔ cup hot water
5–10ml/1–2 tsp redcurrant jelly
salt and ground black pepper

For the stuffing
25g/1oz/2 tbsp butter
50g/2oz bacon, finely chopped
2 large onions, finely chopped
75g/3oz/1½ cups fresh
 white breadcrumbs
30ml/2 tbsp chopped fresh sage
5ml/1 tsp chopped fresh thyme
10ml/2 tsp grated lemon rind
1 small egg, beaten

1 Preheat the oven to 220°C/425°F/Gas 7. To make the stuffing, melt the butter in a heavy pan and fry the bacon until it begins to brown. Add the onions and cook gently until softened, but do not allow to brown. Mix with the breadcrumbs, sage, thyme, lemon rind and egg, then season well with salt and pepper.

2 Cut the rind off the joint of pork in one piece and score it well. Place the pork fat-side down and season. Add a layer of stuffing, then roll up and tie neatly. Lay the rind over the pork and rub in 5ml/1 tsp salt. Roast for 2–2½ hours, basting occasionally. Reduce the temperature to 190°C/375°F/Gas 5 after 20 minutes. Shape the remaining stuffing into balls and add to the roasting pan for the last 30 minutes.

3 Remove the rind from the pork. Increase the temperature to 220°C/425°F/Gas 7 and roast the rind for a further 20–25 minutes, until crisp. Mix the breadcrumbs and sage and press them into the pork fat. Cook the pork for 10 minutes, then cover and set aside in a warm place for 15–20 minutes.

4 Remove all but 30–45ml/2–3 tbsp of the fat from the pan. Place over medium heat, stir in the flour, the cider and water. Cook for 10 minutes. Strain the gravy into a clean pan, add the jelly and cook for 5 minutes. Serve with the pork and crackling.

Stir-fried Pork Energy 278kcal/1162kJ; Protein 27.5g; Carbohydrate 7.8g, of which sugars 7.4g; Fat 15.4g, of which saturates 8.2g; Cholesterol 105mg; Calcium 42mg; Fibre 1.2g; Sodium 154mg.
Roast Pork Energy 446Kcal/1874kJ; Protein 52.8g; Carbohydrate 26.4g, of which sugars 5.1g; Fat 15.1g, of which saturates 6g; Cholesterol 185mg; Calcium 76mg; Fibre 1.7g; Sodium 479mg.

Ruby Bacon Chops

This dish can be prepared with minimal effort, yet still looks impressive.

4 lean bacon loin chops
45ml/3 tbsp redcurrant jelly
ground black pepper
fresh vegetables, to serve

Serves 4

1 ruby grapefruit

1 Cut off all the peel and pith from the grapefruit with a sharp knife. Cut out the segments, catching the juice in a bowl.

2 Fry the bacon chops in a non-stick frying pan without fat, turning them once, until golden. Add the reserved grapefruit juice and redcurrant jelly to the pan and stir until the jelly has melted. Add the grapefruit segments, season with pepper and serve hot with fresh vegetables.

Beef Strips with Orange & Ginger

Stir-frying is a good way of cooking with the minimum of fat, so it's one of the quickest as well as one of the healthiest ways to cook.

grated rind and juice of
  1 orange
15ml/1 tbsp soy sauce
1 tbsp cornflour (cornstarch)
2.5cm/1in fresh root ginger,
  finely chopped
10ml/2 tsp sesame oil
1 carrot, cut into small strips
2 spring onions, (scallions), sliced

Serves 4

450g/1lb rump (round) steak, cut
  into strips

1 Place the beef strips in a bowl and sprinkle with the orange rind and juice. Leave to marinate for 30 minutes. Drain the liquid and reserve, then mix the meat with the soy sauce, cornflour and ginger.

2 Heat the oil in a wok and stir-fry the beef for 1 minute. Add the carrot and stir-fry for 2–3 minutes. Stir in the spring onions and the reserved liquid, then boil, stirring, until thickened. Serve.

Beef & Mushroom Burgers

It's worth making your own burgers to cut down on fat and for the added flavour – in this recipe the meat is extended with mushrooms for extra fibre.

50g/2oz/1 cup fresh
  white breadcrumbs
5ml/1 tsp dried mixed herbs
15ml/1 tbsp tomato
  purée (paste)
plain (all-purpose) flour,
  for shaping
salt and ground black pepper

Serves 4

1 small onion, coarsely chopped
150g/5oz/2 cups small
  cup mushrooms
450g/1lb lean minced
  (ground) beef

To serve

tomato or barbecue relish
salad
burger buns or pitta bread

1 Put the onion and mushrooms in a food processor and process until finely chopped. Add the beef, breadcrumbs, herbs and tomato purée and season with salt and pepper. Process until the mixture binds together but still has some texture.

2 Scrape the mixture into a bowl and divide into 8–10 pieces. Flour your hands and shape the pieces into patties. Place on a baking sheet or large plate, cover with clear film (plastic wrap) and chill in the refrigerator for 30 minutes.

3 Cook the burgers in a non-stick frying pan, without any added fat, or under a preheated grill (broiler), turning once, for 12–15 minutes, until evenly cooked. Serve immediately with relish and salad, in burger buns or pitta bread.

Cook's Tip

Home-made burgers have a looser texture than the store-bought variety. It is useful to chill them before cooking as this helps the burgers to firm up, so they are less likely to disintegrate when turned during cooking. If you are grilling (broiling) them, don't transfer them from the baking sheet to the grill (broiler) pan.

Bacon Energy 328kcal/1379kJ; Protein 47.7g; Carbohydrate 10.5g, of which sugars 10.5g; Fat 10.9g, of which saturates 3.5g; Cholesterol 129mg; Calcium 20mg; Fibre 0.5g; Sodium 92mg.
Beef Strips Energy 212kcal/885kJ; Protein 25.7g; Carbohydrate 3.8g, of which sugars 0.3g; Fat 10.5g, of which saturates 4.3g; Cholesterol 65mg; Calcium 7mg; Fibre 0g; Sodium 341mg.
Burgers Energy 266kcal/1115kJ; Protein 27.6g; Carbohydrate 14.3g, of which sugars 3.7g; Fat 11.3g, of which saturates 4.8g; Cholesterol 63mg; Calcium 44mg; Fibre 1.5g; Sodium 209mg.

Beef Paprika with Roasted Peppers

This dish is perfect for family suppers – and roasting the peppers gives an added dimension.

Serves 4

30ml/2 tbsp olive oil
675g/1½lb braising steak, cut into 4cm/1½in dice
2 onions, chopped
1 garlic clove, crushed
15g/½oz/2 tbsp plain (all-purpose) flour
15ml/1 tbsp paprika, plus extra to garnish
400g/14oz can chopped tomatoes
2 red (bell) peppers, seeded and halved
150ml/¼ pint/⅔ cup crème fraîche
salt and ground black pepper
buttered noodles, to serve

1 Preheat the oven to 140°C/275°F/Gas 1. Heat the oil in a large flameproof casserole over medium heat. Add the meat, in batches, and cook, stirring frequently until evenly browned all over. Remove the meat from the casserole using a slotted spoon and set aside.

2 Add the onions and garlic and cook over low heat, stirring occasionally, for about 5 minutes, until softened but not coloured. Stir in the flour and paprika and cook, stirring constantly, for a further 1–2 minutes.

3 Return the meat and any juices that have collected on the plate to the casserole, then add the chopped tomatoes. Season with salt and pepper. Bring to the boil, stirring constantly, then cover with a tight-fitting lid and cook in the oven for 2½ hours.

4 Meanwhile, place the peppers, skin-side up, on a grill (broiler) rack and grill (broil) until the skins have blistered and charred. Cool, then peel off the skins. Cut the flesh into strips and add to the casserole. Re-cover the casserole and cook for a further 15–30 minutes, or until the meat is tender.

5 Stir in the crème fraîche and sprinkle with a little paprika. Serve hot with buttered noodles.

Rich Beef Casserole

Use a full-bodied red wine such as a Burgundy to create the flavoursome sauce in this casserole.

Serves 4–6

900g/2lb braising steak steak, cut into cubes
2 onions, coarsely chopped
1 bouquet garni
6 black peppercorns
15ml/1 tbsp red wine vinegar
1 bottle red wine
45–60ml/3–4 tbsp olive oil
3 celery sticks, thickly sliced
50g/2oz/½ cup plain (all-purpose) flour
300ml/½ pint/1¼ cups beef stock
30ml/2 tbsp tomato purée (paste)
2 garlic cloves, crushed
175g/6oz chestnut (cremini) mushrooms, halved
400g/14oz can artichoke hearts, drained and halved
chopped fresh parsley and thyme, to garnish

1 Put the meat, onions, bouquet garni, peppercorns, vinegar and wine in a bowl. Cover with clear film (plastic wrap) and leave to marinate in the refrigerator overnight.

2 The next day, preheat the oven to 160°C/325°F/Gas 3. Drain the meat, reserving the marinade, and pat dry. Heat the oil in a large flameproof casserole. Add the meat and onions, in batches, and cook, stirring frequently, until the meat is evenly browned, adding a little more oil if necessary. Remove and set aside. Add the celery to the casserole and cook, stirring frequently, until browned, then remove and set aside.

3 Sprinkle the flour into the casserole and cook, stirring constantly, for 1 minute. Gradually add the reserved marinade and the stock, and bring to the boil, stirring constantly. Return the meat, onions and celery to the casserole, then stir in the tomato purée and garlic.

4 Cover the casserole with a tight-fitting lid and cook in the oven for about 2¼ hours. Stir in the mushrooms and artichokes, cover again and cook for a further 15 minutes, until the meat is tender. Garnish with parsley and thyme, and serve hot with creamy mashed potatoes, if you like.

Beef Paprika Energy 562kcal/2338kJ; Protein 41.7g; Carbohydrate 16.5g, of which sugars 12.1g; Fat 37g, of which saturates 17.6g; Cholesterol 140mg; Calcium 62mg; Fibre 3.2g; Sodium 130mg.
Beef Casserole Energy 457kcal/1905kJ; Protein 36.8g; Carbohydrate 12.2g, of which sugars 4.7g; Fat 20g, of which saturates 6.5g; Cholesterol 87mg; Calcium 77mg; Fibre 2.3g; Sodium 169mg.

Beef Casserole & Dumplings

A traditional English recipe, this delicious casserole is topped with light herbed dumplings for a filling meal.

Serves 4
15ml/1 tbsp oil
450g/1lb minced (ground) beef
16 button (pearl) onions
2 carrots, thickly sliced
2 celery sticks, thickly sliced
25g/1oz/¼ cup plain (all-purpose) flour

600ml/1 pint/2½ cups beef stock
salt and ground black pepper
broccoli florets, to serve (optional)

For the dumplings
115g/4oz/1 cup shredded vegetable suet
50g/2oz/½ cup self-raising (self-rising) flour
15ml/1 tbsp chopped fresh parsley

1 Preheat the oven to 180°C/350°F/Gas 4. Heat the oil in a flameproof casserole over medium heat. Add the beef and cook, stirring frequently to break up the meat, for 5 minutes, until brown and sealed.

2 Add the onions and cook, stirring occasionally, for 5 minutes, until softened but not coloured.

3 Stir in the carrots, celery and flour and cook, stirring constantly, for 1 minute.

4 Gradually stir in the beef stock, season to taste with salt and pepper and bring to the boil. Cover with a tight-fitting lid and cook in the oven for 1¼ hours.

5 For the dumplings, mix together the suet, flour and parsley in a bowl. Stir in sufficient cold water to form a smooth dough and knead lightly.

6 Roll the dumpling mixture into eight equal-size balls between the palms of your hands and place them around the top of the casserole. Return the casserole, uncovered, to the oven for a further 20 minutes, until the dumplings are cooked. Serve with broccoli florets, if you like.

Beef in Guinness

Guinness gives this stew a deep, rich flavour. Use Beamish or another stout if you prefer.

Serves 6
900g/2lb braising steak, cut into 4cm/1½in dice
plain (all-purpose) flour, for coating
45ml/3 tbsp vegetable oil
1 large onion, sliced

1 carrot, thinly sliced
2 celery sticks, thinly sliced
10ml/2 tsp sugar
5ml/1 tsp English (hot) mustard powder
15ml/1 tbsp tomato purée (paste)
2.5 x 7.5cm/1 x 3in strip orange rind
1 bouquet garni
600ml/1 pint/2½ cups Guinness
salt and ground black pepper

1 Toss the beef in flour to coat, shaking off any excess. Heat 30ml/2 tbsp of the oil in a large shallow pan over medium heat. Add the beef, in batches, and cook, stirring frequently, for 8–10 minutes, until lightly browned. Transfer to a bowl.

2 Add the remaining oil to the pan and lower the heat. Add the onion and cook, stirring occasionally, for about 8 minutes, until lightly browned. Add the carrot and celery and cook, stirring occasionally, for a further 5 minutes.

3 Stir in the sugar, mustard, tomato purée, orange rind and Guinness, season with salt and pepper, add the bouquet garni and bring to the boil.

4 Return the meat and any juices in the bowl to the pan. Add water, if necessary, so that the meat is covered. Cover the pan with a tight-fitting lid and simmer over low heat for 2–2½ hours, until the meat is very tender.

Cook's Tip
Like most stews, this can be prepared up to 2 days ahead and stored in the refrigerator, once cooled. The flavours and richness will intensify during this time.

Beef Casserole Energy 619kcal/2567kJ; Protein 25.3g; Carbohydrate 25.5g, of which sugars 6.9g; Fat 46.8g, of which saturates 21.2g; Cholesterol 68mg; Calcium 68mg; Fibre 2.7g; Sodium 117mg.
Beef in Guiness Energy 367kcal/1529kJ; Protein 35.3g; Carbohydrate 6.9g, of which sugars 5.7g; Fat 19.6g, of which saturates 6.4g; Cholesterol 87mg; Calcium 32mg; Fibre 1.2g; Sodium 119mg.

Peppered Steaks with Madeira

This is a really easy dish for special occasions. Mixed peppercorns have an excellent flavour, although black pepper will do.

Serves 4

15ml/1 tbsp mixed dried peppercorns (green, pink and black)

4 fillet (beef tenderloin) or sirloin steaks (about 175g/6oz each)
15ml/1 tbsp olive oil, plus extra oil for pan-frying
1 garlic clove, crushed
60ml/4 tbsp Madeira
90ml/6 tbsp beef stock
150ml/¼ pint/⅔ cup double (heavy) cream
salt

1 Finely crush the peppercorns using a spice grinder, coffee grinder or mortar and pestle, then press them evenly on to both sides of the steaks.

2 Place the steaks in a shallow non-metallic dish, then add the olive oil, garlic and Madeira. Cover the dish with clear film (plastic wrap) and leave to marinate in a cold place or the refrigerator for at least 4–6 hours, or preferably overnight for a more intense flavour.

3 Remove the steaks from the dish, reserving the marinade. Brush a little olive oil over a large heavy frying pan and heat until it is hot.

4 Add the steaks to the pan and cook over high heat, according to taste. Allow about 3 minutes' cooking time per side for a medium steak or 2 minutes per side for rare. Remove the steaks from the frying pan and keep them warm.

5 Add the reserved marinade and the beef stock to the pan and bring to the boil, then leave the sauce to bubble gently until it is well reduced.

6 Add the double cream to the pan, season with salt to taste, and stir until the sauce has thickened slightly. Place the peppered steaks on warmed plates and serve immediately with the sauce handed separately.

Cheese Pasta Bolognese

If you like lasagne, you will love this dish. It is especially popular with children too.

Serves 4

30ml/2 tbsp olive oil
1 onion, chopped
1 garlic clove, crushed
1 carrot, diced
2 celery sticks, chopped
2 rashers (strips) streaky (fatty) bacon, finely chopped
5 button (white) mushrooms, chopped
450g/1lb lean minced (ground) beef

120ml/4fl oz/½ cup red wine
15ml/1 tbsp tomato purée (paste)
200g/7oz can chopped tomatoes
fresh thyme sprig
225g/8oz/2 cups dried spaghetti
300ml/½ pint/1¼ cups milk
25g/1oz/2 tbsp butter
25g/1oz/¼ cup plain (all-purpose) flour
150g/5oz/ mozzarella cheese, diced
60ml/4 tbsp freshly grated Parmesan cheese
salt and ground black pepper
fresh basil sprigs, to garnish

1 Heat the oil in a pan over low heat. Add the onion, garlic, carrot and celery and cook, stirring occasionally, for 5 minutes, until softened. Add the bacon and cook for 3–4 minutes. Add the mushrooms and cook for 2 minutes. Add the beef and cook, stirring frequently, for 5–6 minutes, until well browned.

2 Add the wine, tomato purée, 45ml/3 tbsp water, the tomatoes and thyme sprig. Bring to the boil, cover, and simmer gently for 30 minutes.

3 Preheat the oven to 200°C/400°F/Gas 6. Cook the spaghetti. Meanwhile, place the milk, butter and flour in a pan and heat gently, whisking until thickened. Stir in the mozzarella and half the Parmesan. Season with salt and pepper.

4 Drain the spaghetti and stir into the cheese sauce. Uncover the Bolognese sauce and boil rapidly for 2 minutes. Spoon the sauce into an ovenproof dish, top with the spaghetti mixture and sprinkle with the remaining Parmesan. Bake for 25 minutes, or until golden. Once out of the oven, stir well and garnish with basil. Serve hot.

Steaks Energy 471kcal/1956kJ; Protein 41.8g; Carbohydrate 2.5g, of which sugars 2.5g; Fat 30.8g, of which saturates 16.4g; Cholesterol 141mg; Calcium 28mg; Fibre 0g; Sodium 131mg.
Bolognese Energy 806kcal/3369kJ; Protein 46.1g; Carbohydrate 54.6g, of which sugars 9.6g; Fat 44.1g, of which saturates 21.1g; Cholesterol 122mg; Calcium 461mg; Fibre 3.3g; Sodium 503mg.

Stilton Burgers

This tasty recipe contains a delicious surprise: encased in the crunchy burger is lightly melted Stilton cheese.

Serves 4

450g/1lb minced (ground) beef
1 onion, finely chopped
1 celery stick, chopped
5ml/1 tsp mixed dried herbs
5ml/1 tsp mustard
50g/2oz/½ cup crumbled
  Stilton cheese
salt and ground black pepper
salad and mashed potatoes,
  to serve

1 Preheat the grill (broiler). Place the minced beef in a bowl with the chopped onion and celery. Mix together, then season with salt and pepper.

2 Stir in the herbs and mustard, bringing all the ingredients together to form a firm mixture.

3 Divide the mixture into eight equal portions and roll them into balls between the palms of your hands. Place four on a chopping board and flatten each one slightly into a round.

4 Divide the crumbled cheese between the four rounds, placing a portion in the centre of each. Flatten the remaining balls into rounds and place on top, covering the cheese. Gently mould the mixture together, encasing the crumbled cheese completely, and shape into four burgers.

5 Grill (broil) under medium heat, turning once, for 10 minutes, or until cooked through. Serve with mashed potatoes and a freshly made salad, if liked.

> **Cook's Tip**
> These burgers could be made with minced (ground) lamb or pork for a change, but make sure that they are thoroughly cooked and not pink inside.

Steak, Kidney & Mushroom Pie

If you prefer, you can omit the kidneys from this pie and substitute more braising steak in their place.

Serves 4

30ml/2 tbsp sunflower oil
1 onion, chopped
115g/4oz bacon, finely chopped
500g/1¼ lb braising steak, diced
25g/1oz/¼ cup plain (all-
  purpose) flour
115g/4oz lamb's kidneys
large bouquet garni
400ml/14fl oz/1¾ cups beef
  stock
115g/4oz button
  (white) mushrooms
225g/8oz puff pastry dough,
  thawed if frozen
beaten egg, to glaze
salt and ground black pepper

1 Preheat the oven to 160°C/325°F/Gas 3. Heat the oil in a heavy pan over low heat. Add the onion and bacon and cook, stirring occasionally, for about 8 minutes, until lightly browned.

2 Toss the steak in the flour. Stir the meat into the pan, in batches, and cook, stirring frequently, until evenly browned. Toss the kidneys in flour, add to the pan with the bouquet garni and cook briefly, stirring occasionally, until browned.

3 Transfer the meat and onions to a casserole, pour in the stock, cover with a tight-fitting lid and cook in the oven for 2 hours. Remove the casserole from the oven, stir in the mushrooms, season with salt and pepper and leave to cool.

4 Preheat the oven to 220°C/425°F/Gas 7. Roll out the pastry to 2cm/¾in larger than the top of a 1.2 litre/2 pint/5 cup pie dish. Cut off a pastry strip and fit it around the dampened rim of the dish. Brush the pastry strip with water.

5 Tip the meat mixture into the dish. Lay the pastry over the dish, press the edges together to seal, then knock them up with the back of a knife. Make a small slit in the pastry, brush with beaten egg and bake for 20 minutes. Lower the oven temperature to 180°C/350°F/Gas 4 and bake for a further 20 minutes, until the pastry is risen, golden and crisp.

Burgers Energy 519kcal/2177kJ; Protein 32.2g; Carbohydrate 42.8g, of which sugars 2.8g; Fat 25.5g, of which saturates 10.8g; Cholesterol 76mg; Calcium 156mg; Fibre 1.6g; Sodium 632mg.
Steak Energy 597kcal/2488kJ; Protein 42.5g; Carbohydrate 27g, of which sugars 1.7g; Fat 36.7g, of which saturates 7.5g; Cholesterol 178mg; Calcium 57mg; Fibre 0.7g; Sodium 742mg.

Beef Stew with Red Wine

A slow-cooked casserole of tender beef in a red wine and plum tomato sauce.

Serves 6

75ml/5 tbsp olive oil
1.2kg/2½lb braising steak, cut into 3cm/1½in cubes
1 onion, very thinly sliced
2 carrots, chopped
45ml/3 tbsp finely chopped fresh parsley
1 garlic clove, chopped
1 bay leaf
a few fresh thyme sprigs
pinch of freshly ground nutmeg
250ml/8fl oz/1 cup red wine
400g/14oz can plum tomatoes, chopped, with their juice
120ml/4fl oz/½ cup beef or chicken stock
about 15 black olives, pitted and halved
salt and ground black pepper
1 large red (bell) pepper, seeded and cut into strips

1 Preheat the oven to 180°C/350°F/Gas 4. Heat 45ml/3 tbsp of the oil in a large heavy flameproof casserole over medium heat. Add the meat, in batches, and cook, stirring frequently, until evenly browned all over. Remove to a side plate as the meat is browned and set aside until needed.

2 Add the remaining oil, the onion and carrots to the casserole and lower the heat. Cook, stirring occasionally, for about 5 minutes, until the onion has softened but not coloured. Add the parsley and garlic and cook, stirring occasionally, for a further 3–4 minutes.

3 Return the meat to the casserole, increase the heat and stir well to mix the vegetables with the meat. Stir in the bay leaf, thyme and nutmeg. Add the wine, bring to the boil and cook, stirring constantly, for 4–5 minutes. Stir in the tomatoes, stock and olives and mix well. Season to taste with salt and pepper. Cover the casserole with a tight-fitting lid and transfer to the oven. Bake for 1½ hours.

4 Remove the casserole from the oven. Stir in the strips of pepper. Return the casserole to the oven and cook, uncovered, for 30 minutes more, or until the beef is tender.

Cottage Pie

This traditional dish is a favourite with adults and children alike.

Serves 4

30ml/2 tbsp vegetable oil
1 onion, finely chopped
1 carrot, finely chopped
115g/4oz chopped mushrooms
500g/1¼lb lean minced (ground) braising steak
300ml/½ pint/1¼ cups brown veal stock or water
15g/½oz/2 tbsp plain (all-purpose) flour
1 bay leaf
10–15ml/2–3 tsp Worcestershire sauce
15ml/1 tbsp tomato purée (paste)
675g/1½lb potatoes, boiled
25g/1oz/2 tbsp butter
45ml/3 tbsp hot milk
15ml/1 tbsp chopped fresh tarragon
salt and ground black pepper

1 Heat the oil in a pan over low heat. Add the onion, carrot and mushrooms and cook, stirring occasionally, for about 10 minutes, until the onion is softened and lightly browned. Stir the beef into the pan and cook, stirring to break up the lumps, for about 8 minutes, until lightly browned.

2 Blend a few spoonfuls of the stock or water with the flour, then stir into the pan. Stir in the remaining stock or water and bring to a simmer, stirring constantly.

3 Add the bay leaf, Worcestershire sauce and tomato purée, then cover with a tight-fitting lid and cook very gently for 1 hour, stirring occasionally. Uncover towards the end of cooking to allow any excess liquid to evaporate, if necessary.

4 Preheat the oven to 190°C/375°F/Gas 5. Gently heat the potatoes for a couple of minutes, then mash with the butter, milk and seasoning.

5 Add the tarragon to the meat mixture and season to taste with salt and pepper, then pour into a pie dish. Cover the meat with an even layer of mashed potatoes and mark the top of the pie with the prongs of a fork. Bake for about 25 minutes, until golden brown. Serve immediately.

Beef Stew Energy 464kcal/1929kJ; Protein 42.7g; Carbohydrate 4.5g, of which sugars 4.1g; Fat 27.5g, of which saturates 8.3g; Cholesterol 106mg; Calcium 44mg; Fibre 1.8g; Sodium 321mg.
Cottage Pie Energy 281kcal/1179kJ; Protein 7.2g; Carbohydrate 34.6g, of which sugars 6.2g; Fat 13.7g, of which saturates 5.1g; Cholesterol 22mg; Calcium 50mg; Fibre 2.9g; Sodium 132mg.

Pasta Bows with Smoked Salmon

For a quick dish with a touch of luxury, this recipe is hard to beat – a divine combination of creamy smoked salmon sauce and pretty pasta shapes.

Serves 4
6 spring onions (scallions), sliced
50g/2oz/¼ cup butter
90ml/6 tbsp dry white wine or vermouth

450ml/¾ pint/scant 2 cups double (heavy) cream
a pinch of freshly grated nutmeg
225g/8oz smoked salmon
30ml/2 tbsp chopped fresh dill or 15ml/1 tbsp dried dill
freshly squeezed lemon juice
450g/1lb/4 cups dried farfalle
salt and ground black pepper

1 Slice the spring onions finely. Melt the butter in a pan and fry the spring onions for about 1 minute until they begin to soften.

2 Add the wine or vermouth and boil hard to reduce to about 30ml/2 tbsp. Stir in the cream and add salt, pepper and nutmeg to taste. Bring to the boil and simmer for about 2–3 minutes, until slightly thickened.

3 Cut the smoked salmon into 2.5cm/1in squares and stir into the sauce with the dill. Taste and add a little lemon juice. Keep the sauce warm.

4 Bring a large pan of lightly salted water to the boil and cook the pasta until al dente. Drain well and toss with the sauce.

> **Cook's Tip**
> Smoked salmon trimmings are perfectly adequate for this dish.

> **Variation**
> This dish could also be prepared with canned salmon, broken into bitesize pieces, if you prefer.

Pasta with Tuna & Capers

A piquant sauce of tuna, capers, anchovies and fresh basil combines brilliantly with pasta, creating an easy dish full of punchy flavours.

Serves 4
400g/14oz can tuna in oil
30ml/2 tbsp olive oil
2 garlic cloves, crushed

800g/1¾ lb canned chopped tomatoes
6 canned anchovy fillets, drained
30ml/2 tbsp capers in vinegar, drained
30ml/2 tbsp chopped fresh basil
450g/1lb/4 cups dried garganelle, penne or rigatoni
salt and ground black pepper
fresh basil sprigs, to garnish

1 Drain the oil from the tuna into a pan, add the olive oil and heat gently until it stops spitting.

2 Add the garlic and fry until golden. Stir in the tomatoes and simmer for 25 minutes until thickened.

3 Flake the tuna and cut the anchovies in half. Stir into the sauce with the capers and chopped basil. Season to taste with salt and pepper.

4 Bring a large pan of lightly salted water to the boil and cook the pasta until al dente. Drain well and toss with the sauce. Garnish with fresh basil sprigs and serve immediately.

> **Cook's Tip**
> Tubular pasta is particularly good with this sauce as the tasty bits get trapped in the tube cavities. Other hollow shapes, such as conchiglie (shells) and lumache (snails), will also work well.

> **Variation**
> This piquant sauce could be made without the addition of tomatoes – just heat the oil, add the other ingredients and heat through gently before tossing with the pasta.

Tuna & Capers Energy 666kcal/2817kJ; Protein 43.1g; Carbohydrate 89.6g, of which sugars 9.9g; Fat 17.6g, of which saturates 2.8g; Cholesterol 53mg; Calcium 68mg; Fibre 5.3g; Sodium 488mg.
Pasta Bows Energy 1144kcal/4770kJ; Protein 30g; Carbohydrate 86.5g, of which sugars 6.8g; Fat 75.3g, of which saturates 44.8g; Cholesterol 201mg; Calcium 104mg; Fibre 3.5g; Sodium 1165mg.

Cannelloni al Forno

This recipe provides a lighter, healthier alternative to the usual beef-filled, béchamel-coated version.

Serves 4–6

450g/1lb boned chicken breast, skinned and cooked
225g/8oz mushrooms
2 garlic cloves, crushed
30ml/2 tbsp chopped fresh parsley
15ml/1 tbsp chopped fresh tarragon
1 egg, beaten
squeeze of lemon juice
12–18 cannelloni tubes
butter, for greasing
1 jar passata (bottled strained tomatoes)
50g/2oz/scant ¾ cup freshly grated Parmesan cheese
salt and ground black pepper
fresh basil leaves, to garnish

1 Preheat the oven to 200°C/400°F/Gas 6. Place the chicken in a food processor and blend until finely minced. Transfer to a bowl and set aside.

2 Place the mushrooms, garlic, parsley and tarragon in the food processor and blend until finely minced. Beat the mushroom mixture into the chicken with the egg, and season with salt and pepper and lemon juice to taste.

3 Bring a large pan of lightly salted water to the boil and cook the cannelloni until *al dente*. Drain well on a clean dish towel.

4 Place the filling in a piping bag fitted with a large plain nozzle. Use this to fill each tube of cannelloni.

5 Lay the filled cannelloni tightly together in a single layer in a buttered shallow ovenproof dish. Spoon over the passata and sprinkle with Parmesan cheese. Bake in the oven for 30 minutes or until brown and bubbling. Garnish with basil leaves.

> **Cook's Tip**
> *Passata is sieved (strained) ripe tomatoes and is a convenient store-cupboard item. It is available from larger supermarkets.*

Fettuccine all'Alfredo

A classic from Rome, this dish is simply pasta tossed with cream, butter and freshly grated Parmesan cheese. It makes a great supper dish, served with a crisp green salad to cut through the richness.

Serves 4

25g/1oz/2 tbsp butter
150ml/¼ pint/⅔ cup double (heavy) cream, plus 60ml/4 tbsp extra
450g/1lb dried fettuccine
50g/2oz/scant ¾ cup freshly grated Parmesan cheese, plus extra to serve
pinch of freshly grated nutmeg
salt and ground black pepper

1 Place the butter and 150ml/¼ pint/⅔ cup cream in a heavy pan. Bring to the boil, then simmer for 1 minute until the mixture has slightly thickened.

2 Bring a large pan of lightly salted water to the boil and cook the fettuccine until it is *al dente* – it should still be a little firm to the bite.

3 Drain the pasta very thoroughly and return to the pan with the cream sauce.

4 Place the pan on the heat and turn the pasta in the sauce to coat it evenly.

5 Add the remaining cream, the Parmesan cheese, salt and pepper to taste and a little grated nutmeg. Toss until well coated and heated through. Serve immediately with some extra grated Parmesan cheese sprinkled on top.

> **Variations**
> *For a little extra colour, fresh or frozen peas make an attractive addition to the sauce. You could also try stirring in thin strips of ham if you are not catering for vegetarians. The fettuccine ribbons can be replaced by spaghetti very successfully.*

Cannelloni Energy 375kcal/1589kJ; Protein 31.8g; Carbohydrate 51.8g, of which sugars 4.5g; Fat 6g, of which saturates 2.4g; Cholesterol 93mg; Calcium 151mg; Fibre 3.2g; Sodium 308mg.
Fettuccine Energy 674kcal/2830kJ; Protein 19.1g; Carbohydrate 84g, of which sugars 4.4g; Fat 31.4g, of which saturates 18.6g; Cholesterol 77mg; Calcium 198mg; Fibre 3.3g; Sodium 186mg.

Tagliatelle with Gorgonzola Sauce

Gorgonzola, the Italian creamy blue cheese, is used to create a mouthwatering sauce for pasta. Serve with a mixed green salad as a foil to the richness of the dish.

Serves 4

25g/1oz/2 tbsp butter, plus extra
    for tossing the pasta
225g/8oz Gorgonzola cheese
150ml/¼ pint/⅔ cup double
    (heavy) or whipping cream
30ml/2 tbsp dry vermouth
5ml/1 tsp cornflour (cornstarch)
30ml/1 tbsp chopped fresh sage
450g/1lb dried tagliatelle
salt and ground black pepper
sage leaves, to garnish (optional)

1 Melt the butter in a heavy pan (it needs to be thick-based to prevent the cheese from burning). Stir in 175g/6oz/1½ cups crumbled Gorgonzola cheese and stir over very gentle heat for 2–3 minutes, until the cheese has melted.

2 Pour in the cream, vermouth and cornflour, whisking well to amalgamate. Stir in the chopped sage, then season to taste with salt and pepper. Cook, whisking all the time, until the sauce boils and thickens. Set aside.

3 Bring a large pan of lightly salted water to the boil and cook the tagliatelle until *al dente*. Drain well and toss with a little butter to coat evenly.

4 Reheat the sauce gently, whisking well. Divide the pasta among four serving bowls, top with the sauce and sprinkle over the remaining cheese. Garnish with sage leaves, if using, then serve immediately.

> **Cook's Tip**
> *If you do not have vermouth, you can use a good quality dry sherry in its place very successfully. The Gorgonzola can be substituted by another well-flavoured, creamy blue cheese such as Danish Blue or Pipo Crème.*

Tagliatelle with Hazelnut Pesto

Hazelnuts are used instead of pine nuts in this pesto sauce, providing a healthier, lower-fat option.

Serves 4

2 garlic cloves, crushed
25g/1oz fresh basil leaves
25g/1oz/¼ cup chopped
    hazelnuts
200g/7oz/scant 1 cup soft cheese
225g/8oz tagliatelle
ground black pepper

1 Place the garlic, basil, hazelnuts and cheese in a food processor or blender and process to a thick paste.

2 Bring a large pan of lightly salted water to the boil and cook the tagliatelle until *al dente*. Drain well.

3 Spoon the sauce into the hot pasta, tossing until melted. Sprinkle with pepper and serve immediately.

Spaghetti with Tuna Sauce

Tuna is combined with tomatoes, garlic and chilli to make a great piquant sauce for pasta.

Serves 4

225g/8oz dried spaghetti or
    450g/1lb fresh spaghetti
400g/14oz can chopped
    tomatoes
1 garlic clove
425g/15oz canned tuna
4 black olives
2.5ml/½ tsp chilli sauce
    (optional)
salt and ground black pepper

1 Bring a large pan of lightly salted water to the boil and cook the spaghetti until *al dente*. Drain well and keep hot.

2 Place the chopped tomatoes in a pan with the garlic and simmer for 2–3 minutes. Add the tuna, olives and chilli sauce, if using, and heat well. Toss with the spaghetti and heat through. Season to taste with salt and pepper and serve immediately.

Tagliatelle Energy 746kcal/3131kJ; Protein 26.1g; Carbohydrate 86g, of which sugars 5.2g; Fat 34.7g, of which saturates 24.2g; Cholesterol 58mg; Calcium 334mg; Fibre 3.3g; Sodium 750mg.
Tagliatelle with Pesto Energy 392kcal/1642kJ; Protein 12.1g; Carbohydrate 42.2g, of which sugars 2.3g; Fat 20.6g, of which saturates 10.1g; Cholesterol 45mg; Calcium 90mg; Fibre 2.4g; Sodium 169mg.
Spaghetti Energy 413kcal/1748kJ; Protein 36.3g; Carbohydrate 44.8g, of which sugars 5g; Fat 11.2g, of which saturates 1.9g; Cholesterol 53mg; Calcium 36mg; Fibre 2.7g; Sodium 386mg.

Penne with Broccoli & Chilli

Simple to make, yet filled with tasty flavours, this dish is ideal for an easy midweek meal. Try using other pasta shapes, such as fusilli spirals.

Serves 4

350g/12oz/3 cups penne pasta
450g/1lb/4 cups chopped broccoli stems and florets
30ml/2 tbsp stock
1 garlic clove, crushed
1 small red chilli, finely sliced, or 2.5ml/½ tsp chilli sauce
60ml/4 tbsp natural (plain) low-fat yogurt
30ml/2 tbsp toasted pine nuts or cashew nuts
salt and ground black pepper
freshly chopped parsley

1 Bring a large pan of lightly salted water to the boil, add the pasta and return to the boil. Place the broccoli in a steamer basket over the top. Cover and cook for 8–10 minutes, until both are just tender. Drain.

2 Heat the stock in a pan and add the crushed garlic and chilli or chilli sauce. Stir over a low heat for 2–3 minutes.

3 Stir in the broccoli, pasta and yogurt. Season with salt and pepper, then sprinkle with nuts and parsley and serve.

Cook's Tips
• *For the best results, it is important that the broccoli is very fresh – it should be bright green and firm, not limp. Cut the florets into bite-size pieces, removing any woody stem.*
• *To toast pine nuts for sprinkling on top, heat a dry heavy frying pan, add the pine nuts and toss quickly over medium heat until they turn pale golden. Do not allow them to brown, otherwise they will taste bitter.*

Variation
For a milder sauce you could omit the chilli. Instead, add some diced ham with the garlic to give extra flavour and texture.

Linguine with Pesto Sauce

Pesto, the famous Italian basil sauce, originates in Liguria, where the sea breezes are said to give the local basil a particularly fine flavour. Pesto is traditionally made with a pestle and mortar, but it is easier to make in a food processor or blender.

Serves 5–6

65g/2½ oz fresh basil leaves
3–4 garlic cloves, peeled
45ml/3 tbsp pine nuts
75ml/5 tbsp extra virgin olive oil
50g/2oz/scant ¾ cup freshly grated Parmesan cheese
60ml/4 tbsp freshly grated Pecorino cheese
salt and ground black pepper
500g/1¼ lb linguine pasta

1 Place the basil leaves, garlic cloves, pine nuts, 2.5ml/½ tsp salt and olive oil in a food processor or blender and process until smooth. Transfer to a bowl.

2 Stir in the Parmesan and Pecorino cheeses and stir to combine thoroughly. Season to taste with salt and pepper.

3 Bring a large pan of lightly salted water the boil and cook the linguine until it is *al dente*. Just before draining the pasta, take out about 60ml/4 tbsp of the cooking water and stir it into the pesto sauce.

4 Drain the pasta and toss with the sauce. Serve at once, with extra cheese if wished.

Cook's Tip
• *Pecorino cheese is not as widely available as Parmesan. If you cannot find it, use all Parmesan instead. For the best flavour, buy a piece of Parmesan and grate it yourself.*
• *Pesto sauce is handy to have as a standby in the freezer. It's a good idea to freeze the pesto in an ice cube tray so that you can use as little or as much as you like. Freeze at the end of step 1, before adding the cheese.*

Penne Energy 397kcal/1678kJ; Protein 17.3g; Carbohydrate 68.3g, of which sugars 6g; Fat 7.9g, of which saturates 0.8g; Cholesterol 0mg; Calcium 114mg; Fibre 5.6g; Sodium 24mg.
Linguine Energy 476kcal/2000kJ; Protein 17.6g; Carbohydrate 56.1g, of which sugars 2.9g; Fat 21.7g, of which saturates 5.6g; Cholesterol 18mg; Calcium 258mg; Fibre 2.6g; Sodium 217mg.

Rigatoni with Garlic Crumbs

A spicy treat: pasta tubes coated in a chilli-flavoured tomato sauce, topped with crunchy garlicky crumbs.

Serves 4–6
45ml/3 tbsp olive oil
2 shallots, chopped
8 streaky (fatty) bacon rashers
  (strips), chopped
10ml/2 tsp crushed dried chillies
400g/14oz can chopped
  tomatoes with herbs
6 slices white bread, crusts
  removed
115g/4oz/½ cup butter
2 garlic cloves, chopped
450g/1lb/4 cups dried rigatoni
salt and ground black pepper
fresh herbs sprigs, to garnish

1 Heat the oil in a pan and fry the shallots and bacon gently for 6–8 minutes until golden. Add the dried chillies and chopped tomatoes, half-cover with a lid and simmer for about 20 minutes, stirring occasionally.

2 Meanwhile, place the bread in a blender or food processor and process to fine crumbs. Heat the butter in a frying pan and stir-fry the garlic and breadcrumbs until golden and crisp. (Be careful not to let the crumbs catch and burn.)

3 Bring a large pan of lightly salted water to the boil and cook the rigatoni until *al dente*. Drain well.

4 Toss the pasta with the tomato sauce and divide among four bowls. Sprinkle with the crumbs and garnish with herbs.

Cook's Tip
To keep the breadcrumbs crisp and dry after frying, drain them on kitchen paper and place in a low oven until ready to use.

Variation
To make this dish suitable for vegetarians, leave out the bacon, or replace it with sliced mushrooms.

Stir-fried Vegetables with Pasta

This is a colourful oriental-style dish, easily prepared using pasta instead of Chinese noodles.

Serves 4
1 carrot
175g/6oz small courgettes
  (zucchini)
175g/6oz runner or other green
  beans
175g/6oz baby corn on the cob
450g/1lb dried ribbon pasta such
  as tagliatelle
pinch of salt
30ml/2 tbsp corn oil, plus extra
  for tossing the pasta
1cm/½ in piece fresh root ginger,
  peeled and finely chopped
2 garlic cloves, finely chopped
90ml/6 tbsp yellow bean sauce
6 spring onions (scallions), sliced
  into 2.5cm/1in lengths
30ml/2 tbsp dry sherry
5ml/1 tsp sesame seeds

1 Slice the carrot and courgettes diagonally into chunks. Slice the beans diagonally, then cut the baby corn on the cob diagonally in half.

2 Bring a large pan of lightly salted water to the boil and cook the pasta until *al dente*. Drain, then rinse under hot water. Toss in a little oil.

3 Heat 30ml/2 tbsp oil in a wok or frying pan until smoking and add the ginger and garlic. Stir-fry for 30 seconds, then add the carrots, courgettes and beans.

4 Stir-fry for 3–4 minutes then stir in the yellow bean sauce. Stir-fry for 2 minutes, add the spring onions, sherry and pasta and stir-fry for a further 1 minute until piping hot. Sprinkle with sesame seeds and serve immediately.

Variation
You can vary the vegetables as you wish. Try strips of red (bell) pepper, sugar snap peas, button mushrooms and beansprouts. Make sure the wok is very hot before adding the vegetables.

Rigatoni Energy 645kcal/2708kJ; Protein 18.4g; Carbohydrate 75g, of which sugars 6.1g; Fat 32.3g, of which saturates 14.1g; Cholesterol 65mg; Calcium 68mg; Fibre 3.5g; Sodium 771mg.
Stir-fried Vegetables Energy 560kcal/2370kJ; Protein 21.6g; Carbohydrate 100g, of which sugars 8g; Fat 9.1g, of which saturates 1.3g; Cholesterol 0mg; Calcium 86mg; Fibre 7.5g; Sodium 513mg.

Chilli Beef Pizza

Minced beef and red kidney beans combined with oregano, cumin and chillies turn this pizza into a Mexican extravaganza.

Serves 4

1 quantity Basic Pizza Dough (see Basic Pizza Dough, below)
30ml/2 tbsp olive oil
1 red onion, finely chopped
1 garlic clove, crushed
½ red (bell) pepper, seeded and finely chopped
175g/6oz/¾ cup lean minced (ground) beef
2.5ml/½ tsp ground cumin
2 fresh red chillies, seeded and chopped
115g/4oz/scant ½ cup (drained weight) canned red kidney beans, rinsed
1 jar ready-made tomato sauce or pizza topping
15ml/1 tbsp chopped fresh oregano
50g/2oz/½ cup grated mozzarella cheese
75g/3oz/¾ cup grated oak-smoked Cheddar cheese
salt and ground black pepper

1 Preheat the oven to 220°C/425°F/Gas 7. Roll out the pizza dough to a 25–30cm/10–12in circle and place on a greased baking sheet. Push up the edge of the dough to form a thin rim.

2 Heat 15ml/1 tbsp of the oil in a frying pan and gently fry the onion, garlic and pepper until soft. Increase the heat, add the beef and brown well, stirring constantly.

3 Add the cumin and chillies and continue to cook, stirring, for about 5 minutes. Add the kidney beans and season with salt and pepper. Remove from the heat.

4 Spread the tomato sauce over the pizza base. Spoon the beef mixture over the top, then sprinkle with the oregano.

5 Arrange over the mozzarella and Cheddar cheeses on top, then sprinkle with the remaining olive oil. Immediately place the pizza in the oven and bake for about 15–20 minutes, or until the crust is golden brown and the topping is bubbling.

Basic Pizza Dough

Making your own pizza base is easy – and it tastes great.

Makes one 25–30cm/ 10–12in round pizza base

175g/6oz/1½ cups strong white flour
1.25ml/¼ tsp salt
5ml/1 tsp easy-blend (rapid-rise) dried yeast
120–150ml/4–5fl oz/½–¾ cup lukewarm water
15ml/1 tbsp olive oil

1 Sift the flour and salt into a large mixing bowl and stir in the yeast. Make a well in the centre and pour in the water and oil. Mix to a soft dough. Knead the dough on a lightly floured board for 10 minutes until smooth and elastic.

2 Place in a greased bowl, cover with clear film (plastic wrap) and leave to double in size for about 1 hour. Turn out on to a floured surface; knead gently for 2–3 minutes. Use as required.

Ham, Pepper & Mozzarella Pizzas

Succulent roasted peppers, salty proscuitto and creamy mozzarella make a delicious topping for these pizzas.

Serves 2

1 red (bell) pepper
1 yellow (bell) pepper
4 thick slices ciabatta bread
4 slices proscuitto, cut into thick strips
75g/3oz mozzarella cheese
ground black pepper
tiny fresh basil leaves, to garnish

1 Place the peppers skin-side up on a baking sheet and grill (broil), turning them until the skins are evenly charred. Place in a bowl, cover with a cloth and leave for 10 minutes. Peel the skins from the peppers and remove the seeds and cores. Cut the flesh into thick strips.

2 Lightly toast the slices of ciabatta bread on both sides until they are golden.

3 Arrange the strips of pepper on the toasted bread with the strips of proscuitto.

4 Thinly slice the mozzarella and arrange on top. Grind over plenty of pepper. Place under a hot grill (broiler) for 2–3 minutes until the cheese is bubbling.

5 Garnish each pizza with basil leaves and serve immediately.

Cook's Tip
For added flavour, cut a garlic clove in half and rub the cut side over the toasted bread before adding the topping.

Variation
Try using pieces of sun-dried tomato in oil instead of the peppers and use Emmenthal cheese instead of mozzarella.

Chilli Beef Energy 494kcal/2067kJ; Protein 22.7g; Carbohydrate 43.9g, of which sugars 5g; Fat 26.1g, of which saturates 10.6g; Cholesterol 54mg; Calcium 280mg; Fibre 4.1g; Sodium 411mg.
Pizza Dough Energy 696kcal/2944kJ; Protein 16.4g; Carbohydrate 136g, of which sugars 2.6g; Fat 13.3g, of which saturates 1.9g; Cholesterol 0mg; Calcium 245mg; Fibre 5.4g; Sodium 5mg.
Ham, Pepper Energy 466kcal/1965kJ; Protein 26.3g; Carbohydrate 63.6g, of which sugars 14.2g; Fat 13.6g, of which saturates 6.4g; Cholesterol 45mg; Calcium 274mg; Fibre 5.1g; Sodium 1173mg.

Mussel & Leek Pizzas

Serve these lovely little seafood pizzas with a crisp green salad for a light lunch.

Serves 4

450g/1lb live mussels in the shell
120ml/4fl oz/½ cup dry white wine
1 quantity Basic Pizza Dough (see page 71)
15ml/1 tbsp olive oil
50g/2oz Gruyère cheese
50g/2oz mozzarella cheese
2 small leeks, thinly sliced
salt and ground black pepper

1 Preheat the oven to 220°C/425°F/Gas 7. Place the mussels in a bowl of cold water to soak, then scrub well. Remove the beards, and discard any mussels that are open.

2 Place the mussels in a pan. Pour over the dry white wine, cover with a tight-fitting lid and cook over high heat, shaking the pan occasionally, for 5–10 minutes until the mussels open.

3 Drain off the cooking liquid. Remove the mussels from their shells, discarding any that remain closed. Leave to cool.

4 Divide the dough into four pieces and roll out each one on a lightly floured surface to a 13cm/5in circle. Place well apart on two greased baking sheets, then push up the dough edges to form a thin rim around the dough circles.

5 Brush the pizza bases with the oil. Grate the cheeses and sprinkle half evenly over the bases. Arrange the leeks over the cheese. Bake for 10 minutes, then remove from the oven.

6 Arrange the mussels on top. Season with salt and pepper and sprinkle over the remaining cheese. Bake for a further 5–10 minutes until crisp and golden. Serve immediately.

Cook's Tip
Frozen or canned mussels can also be used but will give a different flavour and texture to these pizzettes.

Wild Mushroom Pizzas

With their delicate earthy flavour, wild mushrooms make a delicious topping for these little pizzas. Serve as an unusual starter or for a stylish light meal.

Serves 4

45ml/3 tbsp olive oil
350g/12oz fresh mixed wild mushrooms, washed and sliced
2 shallots, chopped
2 garlic cloves, finely chopped
30ml/2 tbsp chopped fresh mixed thyme and flat leaf parsley
1 quantity Basic Pizza Dough (see page 71)
40g/1½ oz/generous ¼ cup grated Gruyère cheese
30ml/2 tbsp freshly grated Parmesan cheese
salt and ground black pepper

1 Preheat the oven to 220°C/425°F/Gas 7. Heat 30ml/2 tbsp of the oil in a frying pan and fry the mushrooms, shallots and garlic over medium heat, stirring occasionally, until all the juices have evaporated.

2 Stir in half the herbs and season with salt and pepper then set aside to cool.

3 Divide the dough into four pieces and roll out each one on a lightly floured surface to a 13cm/5in circle. Place well apart on two greased baking sheets, then push up the dough edges to form a thin rim around the dough circles.

4 Brush the pizza bases with the remaining oil and spoon the wild mushrooms on top. Mix together the Gruyère and Parmesan, then sprinkle over the mushroom mixture.

5 Bake the pizza for 15–20 minutes until crisp and golden. Remove from the oven and scatter over the remaining herbs.

Cook's Tip
Fresh wild mushrooms add a distinctive flavour to the topping, but if they are unavailable, a mixture of cultivated mushrooms, such as shiitake, oyster and chestnut, would do just as well.

Mussel & Leek Energy 343kcal/1441kJ; Protein 16.3g; Carbohydrate 35.6g, of which sugars 2g; Fat 13.6g, of which saturates 5.5g; Cholesterol 33mg; Calcium 280mg; Fibre 2.5g; Sodium 214mg.
Mushroom Energy 340kcal/1425kJ; Protein 11.4g; Carbohydrate 35.6g, of which sugars 1.7g; Fat 17.8g, of which saturates 5.5g; Cholesterol 17mg; Calcium 234mg; Fibre 2.5g; Sodium 160mg.

Farmhouse Pizza

This is the ultimate party pizza. Served cut into fingers, it is ideal for a large and hungry gathering.

Serves 8
90ml/6 tbsp olive oil
225g/8oz button (white) mushrooms, sliced
2 quantities Basic Pizza Dough (see page 71)
1 jar ready-made tomato sauce or pizza topping
300g/10oz mozzarella cheese, thinly sliced
115g/4oz wafer-thin smoked ham slices
6 bottled artichoke hearts in oil, drained and sliced
50g/2oz can anchovy fillets, drained and halved lengthways
10 black olives, pitted and halved
30ml/2 tbsp chopped fresh oregano
15ml/3 tbsp freshly grated Parmesan cheese
ground black pepper

1 Preheat the oven to 220°C/425°F/Gas 7. In a large frying pan, heat 30ml/2 tbsp of the oil. Gently fry the mushrooms for 5 minutes until all the juices have evaporated. Remove from the heat and leave to cool.

2 Roll out the dough on a lightly floured surface to make a 30 x 25cm/12 x 10in rectangle. Transfer to a greased baking sheet, then push up the dough edges to form a thin rim. Brush with 30ml/2 tbsp of the oil.

3 Spread the tomato sauce or pizza topping over the dough, then arrange the sliced mozzarella over the sauce.

4 Scrunch up the ham and arrange on top with the artichoke hearts, mushrooms and anchovies.

5 Dot with the black olives, then sprinkle over the chopped oregano and grated Parmesan. Drizzle over the remaining oil and season to taste with pepper.

6 Bake for about 25 minutes until the pizza crust is crisp and golden. Serve immediately.

Crab & Parmesan Calzonelli

These calzonelli – purses of pizza dough filled with a luxurious creamy crab filling – make attractive and impressive party food.

Makes 10–12
1 quantity Basic Pizza Dough (see page 71)
115g/4oz mixed prepared crab meat, defrosted if frozen
15ml/1 tbsp double (heavy) cream
30ml/2 tbsp freshly grated Parmesan cheese
30ml/2 tbsp chopped fresh parsley
1 garlic clove, crushed
salt and ground black pepper
fresh parsley sprigs, to garnish

1 Preheat the oven to 200°C/400°F/Gas 6. Roll out the pizza dough on a lightly floured surface to 3mm/⅛in thick. Using a 7.5cm/3in plain round pastry cutter, stamp out ten to twelve circles of dough.

2 In a bowl, mix the crab meat with the cream, Parmesan cheese, parsley and garlic. Season to taste with salt and pepper.

3 Spoon a little of the filling on to one half of each circle. Dampen the edges of the dough with water and fold over to enclose the filling.

4 Seal the edges by pressing with a fork. Place well apart on two greased baking sheets. Bake for 10–15 minutes until golden. Garnish with parsley sprigs.

> **Cook's Tip**
> *Make sure that the pizza dough is rolled out thinly and evenly.*

> **Variation**
> *If you prefer, use prawns (shrimp) instead of crab meat. If buying frozen prawns, make sure they are fully defrosted first.*

Farmhouse Energy 412kcal/1725kJ; Protein 17.2g; Carbohydrate 36.4g, of which sugars 2g; Fat 23g, of which saturates 8g; Cholesterol 38mg; Calcium 259mg; Fibre 2.4g; Sodium 822mg.
Calzonelli Energy 84kcal/354kJ; Protein 4.2g; Carbohydrate 11.4g, of which sugars 0.3g; Fat 2.7g, of which saturates 1.1g; Cholesterol 11mg; Calcium 68mg; Fibre 0.6g; Sodium 82mg.

Ham & Mozzarella Calzone

A calzone is a kind of "inside-out" pizza – the dough is on the outside and the filling on the inside. This is particulary good food for eating *al fresco*.

Serves 2

1 quantity Basic Pizza Dough
   (see page 71)
115g/4oz/½ cup ricotta cheese
30ml/2 tbsp freshly grated
   Parmesan cheese
1 egg yolk
30ml/2 tbsp chopped fresh basil
75g/3oz cooked ham, finely
   chopped
75g/3oz mozzarella cheese, cut
   into small dice
olive oil, for brushing
salt and ground black pepper

1 Preheat the oven to 220°C/425°F/Gas 7. Divide the dough in half and roll out each piece on a lightly floured surface to an 18cm/7in circle.

2 In a bowl, mix together the ricotta and Parmesan cheeses, then stir in the egg yolk and basil. Season with salt and pepper.

3 Spread the mixture over half of each circle, leaving a 2.5cm/1in border, then arrange the ham and mozzarella on top.

4 Dampen the edges with water, then fold over the dough to enclose the filling.

5 Press the edges firmly together to seal. Place on two greased baking sheets. Brush with oil and make a small hole in the top of each to allow the steam to escape.

6 Bake for 15–20 minutes until golden. Serve immediately.

Cook's Tips
• *For a vegetarian version, replace the ham with fried mushrooms or chopped cooked spinach.*
• *For a decorative finishing touch, seal the edges of the uncooked dough circles by pressing with a fork.*

Rice with Seeds & Spices

A change from plain boiled rice, this spicy dish makes a colourful accompaniment to curries.

Serves 4

5ml/1 tsp sunflower oil
2.5ml/½ tsp ground turmeric
6 green cardamom pods, lightly
   crushed
5ml/1 tsp coriander seeds, lightly
   crushed
1 garlic clove, crushed
200g/7oz/1 cup basmati rice
400ml/14fl oz/1⅔ cups stock
120ml/4fl oz/½ cup natural
   (plain) yogurt
15ml/1 tbsp toasted sunflower
   seeds
15ml/1 tbsp toasted sesame
   seeds
salt and ground black pepper
fresh coriander (cilantro) leaves, to
   garnish

1 Heat the oil in a non-stick frying pan and fry the spices and garlic for about 1 minute, stirring constantly.

2 Add the rice and stock and stir to mix. Bring to the boil, then cover and simmer for 15 minutes or until just tender.

3 Stir in the yogurt and the toasted sunflower and sesame seeds. Season with salt and pepper to taste and serve immediately, garnished with coriander leaves.

Cook's Tips
• *If you have time, soak the rice for 30 minutes in cold water before cooking.*
• *Although basmati rice gives the best texture and flavour, you could substitute ordinary long grain rice if you prefer.*

Variation
You can always add some unsalted nuts to the dish, to give interesting texture. Shelled pistachios would be a good choice, as they add extra colour, but peanuts, almonds and cashews will all taste just as delicious.

Calzone Energy 686kcal/2877kJ; Protein 34.8g; Carbohydrate 70.2g, of which sugars 3.5g; Fat 31.5g, of which saturates 15.6g; Cholesterol 183mg; Calcium 453mg; Fibre 2.7g; Sodium 769mg.
Rice Energy 248kcal/1035kJ; Protein 6.6g; Carbohydrate 42.2g, of which sugars 2.3g; Fat 5.7g, of which saturates 0.9g; Cholesterol 0mg; Calcium 117mg; Fibre 0.6g; Sodium 27mg.

Louisiana Rice

Minced pork and chicken livers with mixed vegetables make a tasty dish that is a meal in itself.

Serves 4

60ml/4 tbsp vegetable oil
1 small aubergine (eggplant), diced
225g/8oz minced (ground) pork
1 green (bell) pepper, seeded and chopped
2 celery sticks, chopped
1 onion, chopped
1 garlic clove, crushed
5ml/1 tsp cayenne pepper
5ml/1 tsp paprika
5ml/1 tsp ground black pepper
2.5ml/½ tsp salt
5ml/1 tsp dried thyme
2.5ml/½ tsp dried oregano
475ml/16fl oz/2 cups chicken stock
225g/8oz chicken livers, minced (ground)
150g/5oz/¾ cup long grain rice
1 bay leaf
45ml/3 tbsp chopped fresh parsley
celery leaves, to garnish

1 Heat the oil in a frying pan until really hot, then stir-fry the aubergine for about 5 minutes. Add the pork and cook for about 6–8 minutes, until browned, using a wooden spoon to break up any lumps.

2 Add the green pepper, celery, onion, garlic, cayenne pepper, paprika, black pepper, salt, thyme and oregano. Cover and cook over high heat for 5–6 minutes, stirring frequently from the bottom to scrape up and distribute the crispy bits of pork.

3 Pour on the chicken stock and stir, scraping the bottom of the pan clean. Reduce the heat to medium, cover the pan and cook for 6 minutes. Stir in the chicken livers, cook for a further 2 minutes, then stir in the rice and add the bay leaf.

4 Reduce the heat, cover and simmer for about 6–7 minutes more. Turn off the heat and leave to stand for a further 10–15 minutes until the rice is tender.

5 Remove the bay leaf and stir in the chopped parsley. Serve the rice hot, garnished with the celery leaves.

Creole Jambalaya

A fusion of exciting flavours, this colourful dish of chicken thighs, vegetables and rice is very enticing. Serve this nourishing dish surrounded by fresh frisée salad leaves.

Serves 6

4 chicken thighs, boned, skinned and diced
about 300ml/½ pint/1¼ cups chicken stock
1 large green (bell) pepper, seeded and sliced
3 celery sticks, sliced
4 spring onions (scallions), sliced
400g/14oz can tomatoes
5ml/1 tsp ground cumin
5ml/1 tsp ground allspice
2.5ml/½ tsp cayenne pepper
5ml/1 tsp dried thyme
300g/10oz/1½ cups long grain rice
200g/7oz/scant 2 cups peeled, cooked prawns (shrimp)
salt and ground black pepper

1 Fry the chicken in a non-stick pan without fat, turning occasionally, until golden brown.

2 Add 15ml/1 tbsp stock to the pan with the sliced green pepper, celery stick and spring onions. Cook for a few minutes, stirring occasionally, until softened, then stir in the tomatoes, cumin, allspice, cayenne pepper and thyme.

3 Stir in the rice and the remaining stock. Bring to the boil, then reduce the heat, cover tightly and simmer for about 20 minutes, stirring occasionally, until the rice is tender. Add more stock during cooking, if necessary.

4 Stir the peeled prawns into the rice, then return to low heat to warm through the prawns. Season to taste with salt and pepper and serve immediately.

Variation
Traditionally, Jambalayas are made with ham, so try adding 115g/4oz diced cooked ham with the vegetables.

Jambalaya Energy 290kcal/1214kJ; Protein 24g; Carbohydrate 42.1g, of which sugars 2.1g; Fat 2.5g, of which saturates 0.6g; Cholesterol 135mg; Calcium 52mg; Fibre 0.7g; Sodium 134mg.
Louisiana Rice Energy 406kcal/1690kJ; Protein 24.7g; Carbohydrate 35.2g, of which sugars 4.7g; Fat 18.4g, of which saturates 3.8g; Cholesterol 251mg; Calcium 34mg; Fibre 2.1g; Sodium 92mg.

Vegetable Couscous

Harissa is a very fiery Tunisian chilli sauce which is now available ready-made from larger supermarkets.

Serves 4
350g/12oz/2¼ cups couscous
45ml/3 tbsp olive oil
4 baby onions, halved
675g/1½lb fresh mixed vegetables such as carrots, swede (rutabaga), courgettes, cauliflower and sweet potatoes, cubed
2 garlic cloves, crushed
pinch of saffron threads
2.5ml/½ tsp each ground cinnamon and ginger
2.5ml/½ tsp ground turmeric
5ml/1 tsp each ground cumin and coriander

15ml/1 tbsp tomato purée (paste)
450ml/¾ pint/scant 2 cups hot vegetable stock
1 small fennel bulb, quartered
115g/4oz/1 cup cooked or canned chickpeas
50g/2oz/½ cup seedless raisins
30ml/2 tbsp chopped fresh coriander (cilantro)
30ml/2 tbsp chopped fresh flat leaf parsley
salt and ground black pepper

For the spiced sauce
15ml/1 tbsp olive oil
15ml/1 tbsp lemon juice
15ml/1 tbsp chopped fresh coriander (cilantro)
2.5–5ml/½–1 tsp harissa

1 Put the couscous in a bowl, cover with hot water, then drain. Heat the oil in a frying pan and gently fry the onions for 3 minutes. Add the mixed vegetables and fry for 5 minutes. Add the garlic and spices and cook for 1 minute, stirring.

2 Transfer the vegetable mixture to a large deep pan. Stir in the tomato purée, stock, fennel, chickpeas, raisins, chopped coriander and flat leaf parsley. Bring to the boil. Put the couscous into a muslin-lined steamer and place this over the vegetable mixture. Cover and simmer for 20 minutes, or until the vegetables are tender.

3 To make the sauce, put 250ml/8fl oz/1 cup of the vegetable liquid in a bowl and mix with all of the sauce ingredients.

4 Spoon the couscous on to a plate and pile the vegetables on top. Serve at once, handing round the sauce separately.

Risotto with Mushrooms

The addition of wild mushrooms gives a lovely woody flavour to this dish.

Serves 4
25g/1oz dried wild mushrooms, preferably porcini
350ml/12fl oz/1½ cups warm water
900ml/1½ pints/3¾ cups meat or chicken stock
175g/6oz fresh cultivated mushrooms

juice of ½ lemon
75g/3oz/6 tbsp butter
30ml/2 tbsp finely chopped fresh parsley
30ml/2 tbsp olive oil
1 small onion, finely chopped
275g/10oz/1½ cups arborio risotto rice
120ml/4fl oz/½ cup dry white wine
45ml/3 tbsp freshly grated Parmesan cheese
salt and ground black pepper

1 Place the dried mushrooms in a small bowl with the warm water. Leave to soak for at least 40 minutes. Remove the mushrooms and rinse, then filter the soaking water through a sieve (strainer) lined with kitchen paper into a pan. Add the stock and leave to simmer until needed.

2 Slice the fresh mushrooms. Toss with the lemon juice. Melt a third of the butter in a large frying pan. Stir in the mushrooms and cook until they begin to brown. Stir in the parsley, cook for 30 seconds more, then transfer to a side dish.

3 Heat another third of the butter with the olive oil in the mushroom pan and cook the onion until golden. Add the rice and stir for 1–2 minutes. Add all the mushrooms. Pour in the wine and cook until it has evaporated.

4 Add a ladleful of the hot stock and stir gently until it has been absorbed. Continue adding a ladleful of stock at a time, until all the stock has been absorbed and the rice is tender and creamy.

5 Remove the risotto pan from the heat. Stir in the remaining butter and the Parmesan. Grind in a little pepper, and taste again for salt; adjust if necessary. Allow the risotto to rest for 3–4 minutes before serving.

Couscous Energy 444kcal/1855kJ; Protein 9.5g; Carbohydrate 75.1g, of which sugars 24.2g; Fat 13.5g, of which saturates 1.8g; Cholesterol 0mg; Calcium 115mg; Fibre 7.5g; Sodium 131mg.
Risotto Energy 518kcal/2150kJ; Protein 10.6g; Carbohydrate 56.5g, of which sugars 1.2g; Fat 25.2g, of which saturates 12.9g; Cholesterol 51mg; Calcium 161mg; Fibre 0.7g; Sodium 240mg.

Tomato Risotto

This pretty risotto makes a lovely summery meal, served with a chilled white wine.

Serves 4
675g/1½ lb firm ripe tomatoes
50g/2oz/¼ cup butter
1 onion, finely chopped
1.2 litres/2 pints/5 cups vegetable stock
275g/10oz/1½ cups arborio rice
400g/14oz can cannellini beans, drained
50g/2oz/½ cup finely grated Parmesan cheese
salt and ground black pepper
10–12 fresh basil leaves, shredded and freshly grated Parmesan cheese, to serve

1 Halve the tomatoes and scoop out the seeds into a sieve (strainer) placed over a bowl. Press the seeds with a spoon to extract all the juice. Set the juice aside.

2 Grill (broil) the tomatoes skin-side up until evenly charred and blistered. Rub off the skins and dice the flesh.

3 Melt the butter in a large frying pan and cook the onion for 5 minutes until beginning to soften. Add the tomatoes and the reserved juice. Season with salt and pepper, then cook, stirring occasionally, for about 10 minutes. Meanwhile, bring the vegetable stock to the boil in another pan.

4 Add the rice to the tomatoes and stir to coat, then add a ladleful of the stock and stir gently until it has been absorbed. Continue adding a ladleful of stock at a time, until all the stock has been absorbed and the rice is tender and creamy.

5 Stir in the cannellini beans and grated Parmesan and heat through for a few minutes. Just before serving the risotto, sprinkle each portion with shredded basil leaves and Parmesan.

> **Cook's Tip**
> If possible, use plum tomatoes in this dish, as they have a fresh, vibrant flavour and meaty texture.

Grilled Polenta with Peppers

Golden slices of herby polenta taste delicious topped with yellow and red pepper strips, heightened with balsamic vinegar.

Serves 4
2 red (bell) peppers
2 yellow (bell) peppers
115g/4oz/scant 1 cup polenta
25g/1oz/2 tbsp butter
15–30ml/1–2 tbsp mixed chopped herbs such as parsley, thyme and sage
melted butter, for brushing
60ml/4 tbsp olive oil
1–2 garlic cloves, cut into slivers
15ml/1 tbsp balsamic vinegar
salt and ground black pepper
fresh herb sprigs, to garnish

1 Preheat the oven to 200°C/400°F/Gas 6. Place the peppers on a baking sheet and bake for about 20 minutes or until they are beginning to char and blister.

2 Put the charred peppers in a bowl, cover and leave to cool for 10 minutes, then peel off the skins. Remove the seeds and cores, then cut the flesh into strips. Set aside.

3 Bring 600ml/1 pint/2½ cups salted water to the boil in a heavy pan. Trickle in the polenta, beating continuously, then cook gently for 15–20 minutes, stirring occasionally, until the mixture is no longer grainy and comes away from the sides of the pan.

4 Remove the pan from the heat and beat in the butter, chopped herbs and plenty of pepper. Pour the polenta into a pudding bowl, smooth the surface and leave until cold and firm.

5 Turn out the polenta on to a board and cut into thick slices. Brush the polenta slices with melted butter and grill (broil) each side for about 4–5 minutes, until golden brown.

6 Meanwhile, heat the olive oil in a frying pan, add the garlic and peppers and stir-fry for 1–2 minutes. Stir in the balsamic vinegar and season with salt and pepper.

7 Spoon the pepper mixture over the polenta slices and garnish with fresh herb sprigs. Serve immediately.

Risotto Energy 531kcal/2220kJ; Protein 18.4g; Carbohydrate 79.2g, of which sugars 9.8g; Fat 15.9g, of which saturates 9.4g; Cholesterol 39mg; Calcium 252mg; Fibre 8.1g; Sodium 618mg.
Polenta Energy 309kcal/1280kJ; Protein 4.6g; Carbohydrate 32.5g, of which sugars 10.7g; Fat 17.8g, of which saturates 5g; Cholesterol 13mg; Calcium 16mg; Fibre 3.5g; Sodium 45mg.

Red Fried Rice

In this delicious version of egg fried rice, the vibrant colours of red onion, red pepper and cherry tomatoes add lots of eye appeal. An ideal dish for a quick supper.

Serves 2

115g/4oz/¾ cup basmati rice
30ml/2 tbsp groundnut (peanut) oil
1 small red onion, chopped
1 red (bell) pepper, seeded and chopped
225g/8oz cherry tomatoes, halved
2 eggs, beaten
salt and ground black pepper

1 Rinse the rice several times under cold running water. Drain well. Bring a large pan of water to the boil, add the rice and cook for 10–12 minutes.

2 Meanwhile, heat the oil in a wok until very hot and stir-fry the onion and red pepper for 2–3 minutes. Add the cherry tomatoes and stir-fry for a further 2 minutes.

3 Pour in the beaten eggs all at once. Cook for 30 seconds without stirring, then stir to break up the eggs as they set.

4 Drain the cooked rice thoroughly, add to the wok and toss it over the heat with the vegetable and egg mixture for 3 minutes. Season the fried rice with salt and pepper to taste.

Cook's Tips
• *Basmati rice is good for this dish as its slightly crunchy texture complements the softness of the egg.*
• *It is possible to stir-fry in a frying pan, if you don't have a wok. However, the heat will be less evenly distributed and it is harder to toss the ingredients.*

Variation
Add diced cooked ham or chicken with dashes of soy sauce.

Fruity Rice

An oriental-style dressing gives extra piquancy.

Serves 4

115g/4oz/⅔ cup brown or white rice
1 small red (bell) pepper, seeded and diced
200g/7oz can sweetcorn kernels, drained
45ml/3 tbsp sultanas (golden raisins)
225g/8oz can pineapple pieces in fruit juice
15ml/1 tbsp light soy sauce
15ml/1 tbsp sunflower oil
15ml/1 tbsp hazelnut oil
1 garlic clove, crushed
5ml/1 tsp finely chopped fresh root ginger
salt and ground black pepper
4 spring onions (scallions), diagonally sliced, to garnish

1 Bring a large pan of lightly salted water to the boil and cook the rice for about 30 minutes, or until it is just tender. Drain thoroughly, rinse under cold water and drain again. Set aside to cool.

2 Turn the rice into a large serving bowl and add the red pepper, sweetcorn and sultanas. Drain the pineapple pieces, reserving the juice, then add to the rice mixture and toss lightly.

3 Pour the reserved pineapple juice into a clean screw-top jar. Add the soy sauce, sunflower and hazelnut oils, garlic and chopped root ginger. Season to taste with salt and pepper. Close the jar tightly and shake vigorously to combine.

4 Pour the dressing over the salad and toss well. Scatter the spring onions over the top and serve.

Cook's Tip
• *Hazelnut oil gives a distinctive flavour to any salad dressing. Like olive oil, it contains mainly mono-unsaturated fats.*
• *Brown rice is often mistakenly called wholegrain. In fact, the outer husk is completely inedible and is removed from all rice, but the bran layer is left intact on brown rice.*

Red Rice Energy 437kcal/1821kJ; Protein 12.6g; Carbohydrate 57.4g, of which sugars 10.5g; Fat 17.6g, of which saturates 3.1g; Cholesterol 190mg; Calcium 62mg; Fibre 3g; Sodium 85mg.
Fruity Rice Energy 189kcal/797kJ; Protein 3g; Carbohydrate 35.5g, of which sugars 14.4g; Fat 4.8g, of which saturates 0.6g; Cholesterol 0mg; Calcium 18mg; Fibre 1.9g; Sodium 272mg.

Nut Pilaff with Omelette Rolls

This pilaff fuses together a wonderful mixture of textures – soft fluffy rice with crunchy nuts and omelette rolls.

Serves 2
175g/6oz/1 cup basmati rice
15ml/1 tbsp sunflower oil
1 small onion, chopped
1 red (bell) pepper, finely diced
350ml/12fl oz/1½ cups hot
   vegetable stock
2 eggs
25g/1oz/¼ cup salted peanuts
15ml/1 tbsp soy sauce
salt and ground black pepper
fresh parsley sprigs, to garnish

1 Rinse the rice several times under cold running water. Drain thoroughly and set aside.

2 Heat half the oil in a large frying pan and fry the onion and red pepper for 2–3 minutes, then stir in the rice and stock. Bring to the boil, lower the heat slightly and simmer for 10 minutes until the rice is tender.

3 Meanwhile, beat the eggs lightly and season to taste with salt and pepper. Heat the remaining oil in a second large frying pan. Pour in the eggs and tilt the pan to cover the base thinly. Cook the omelette for 1 minute, then flip it over and cook the other side for 1 minute.

4 Slide the omelette on to a clean board and roll it up tightly. Cut the omelette roll into eight slices.

5 Stir the peanuts and the soy sauce into the pilaff and add black pepper to taste. Turn the pilaff into a serving dish, then carefully arrange the omelette rolls on top and garnish with the parsley. Serve immediately.

> **Variation**
> To ring the changes, try salted cashew nuts or toasted flaked almonds instead of the peanuts.

Aubergine Pilaff

This hearty dish is made with bulgur wheat and aubergine, flavoured with fresh mint. It is a perfect choice for a midweek supper as it can be prepared within 15 minutes.

Serves 2
2 aubergines (eggplants)
60–90ml/4–6 tbsp sunflower oil
1 small onion, finely chopped
175g/6oz/1 cup bulgur wheat
450ml/¾ pint/scant 2 cups
   vegetable stock
30ml/2 tbsp pine nuts, toasted
15ml/1 tbsp chopped fresh mint
salt and ground black pepper

For the garnish
lime wedges
lemon wedges
fresh mint sprigs

1 Trim the ends from the aubergines, then slice them lengthways. Cut each slice into neat sticks and then into 1cm/½in dice.

2 Heat 60ml/4 tbsp of the oil in a large heavy frying pan, add the onion and fry over medium heat for 1 minute. Add the the diced aubergine. Increase the heat to high and cook, stirring frequently, for about 4 minutes until just tender. Add the remaining oil if needed.

3 Stir in the bulgur wheat, mixing well, then pour in the vegetable stock. Bring to the boil, then lower the heat and simmer for 10 minutes or until all the liquid has evaporated. Season to taste with salt and pepper.

4 Stir in the pine nuts and mint, then spoon the pilaff on to individual plates. Garnish each portion with lime and lemon wedges. Sprinkle with torn mint leaves for extra colour and serve immediately.

> **Variation**
> Use courgettes (zucchini) instead of aubergine, or for something completely different, substitute pumpkin or acorn squash.

Nut Energy 550kcal/2292kJ; Protein 17.4g; Carbohydrate 80g, of which sugars 8.4g; Fat 17.7g, of which saturates 3.4g; Cholesterol 190mg; Calcium 69mg; Fibre 2.6g; Sodium 609mg.
Aubergine Energy 542kcal/2248kJ; Protein 9.6g; Carbohydrate 52.2g, of which sugars 5.3g; Fat 34g, of which saturates 3.5g; Cholesterol 0mg; Calcium 83mg; Fibre 3.7g; Sodium 7mg.

Gooseberry & Elderflower Cream

Fresh-tasting gooseberries and fragrant elderflowers give this dessert an attractive flavour. For the best presentation, serve the cream in individual dishes, prettily decorated with sprigs of mint.

Serves 4

500g/1¼ lb/4¼ cups
   gooseberries
300ml/½ pint/1¼ cups double
   (heavy) cream
about 115g/4oz/1 cup sifted icing
   (confectioners') sugar, to taste
30ml/2 tbsp elderflower cordial
fresh mint sprigs, to decorate
amaretti, to serve

1 Place the gooseberries in a heavy pan, cover and cook over low heat, shaking the pan occasionally, until the gooseberries are tender. Turn the gooseberries into a bowl, crush them, then leave to cool completely.

2 Whip the cream until soft peaks form, then fold in half of the crushed gooseberries. Sweeten with icing sugar and add elderflower cordial to taste. Sweeten the remaining gooseberries with icing sugar.

3 Layer the cream mixture and the crushed gooseberries in four dessert dishes or tall glasses, then cover and chill. Decorate the dessert with the fresh mint sprigs and serve with amaretti.

Cook's Tips
• If you prefer, the cooked gooseberries can be puréed and sieved (strained) instead of crushed.
• When elderflowers are in season, instead of using the cordial, cook two or three elderflower heads with the gooseberries.

Variation
The elderflower cordial can be replaced by orange flower water to produce a delicately fragrant dessert.

Eton Mess

This dish traditionally forms part of the picnic meals enjoyed by parents and pupils at Eton school. Extremely simple to make, it is a great way to serve succulent strawberries.

Serves 4

500g/1¼ lb/4¼ cups
   strawberries, roughly chopped
45–60ml/3–4 tbsp Kirsch
300ml/½ pint/1¼ cups double
   (heavy) cream
6 small white meringues
fresh mint sprigs, to decorate

1 Put the strawberries in a bowl, sprinkle over the Kirsch, then cover and chill in the refrigerator for 2–3 hours.

2 Whip the cream until soft peaks form, then gently fold in the strawberries with their juices.

3 Crush the meringues into rough chunks, then scatter over the strawberry mixture and fold in gently.

4 Spoon the strawberry mixture into a glass serving bowl, decorate with the fresh mint sprigs and serve immediately.

Cook's Tip
Home-made meringues taste even better. Whisk 3 egg whites until stiff, then gradually whisk in 75g/3oz/6 tbsp caster (superfine) sugar. Fold in another 75g/3oz/6 tbsp caster sugar. Spoon into small mounds on two baking sheets lined with non-stick baking parchment. Bake at 110°C/225°F/Gas ¼ for 2½–3 hours until firm and crisp, but still white.

Variation
If you would prefer to make a less rich version of this dessert, use Greek (US strained plain) or thick and creamy natural (plain) yogurt instead of part or all of the cream. Beat the yogurt gently before adding the strawberries.

Gooseberry Energy 509kcal/2115kJ; Protein 2.7g; Carbohydrate 35.1g, of which sugars 35.1g; Fat 40.8g, of which saturates 25.1g; Cholesterol 103mg; Calcium 87mg; Fibre 3g; Sodium 21mg.
Eton Mess Energy 526kcal/2182kJ; Protein 3.5g; Carbohydrate 32.8g, of which sugars 32.8g; Fat 40.4g, of which saturates 25.1g; Cholesterol 103mg; Calcium 60mg; Fibre 1.4g; Sodium 53mg.

Cranachan

Crunchy toasted oatmeal and soft raspberries combine to give this Scottish dessert a lovely texture, while whisky adds a touch of punchy taste.

Serves 4

60ml/4 tbsp clear honey
45ml/3 tbsp whisky
50g/2oz/¾ cup medium oatmeal
300ml/½ pint/1¼ cups double (heavy) cream
350g/12oz/2 cups raspberries
fresh mint sprigs, to decorate

1 Put the honey in a small pan with the whisky. Heat gently to warm the honey in the whisky, then leave to cool.

2 Preheat the grill (broiler). Spread the oatmeal in a very shallow layer in the grill pan and toast, stirring occasionally, until browned. Leave to cool.

3 Whip the cream in a large bowl until soft peaks form, then gently stir in the oatmeal and the honey and whisky mixture until well combined.

4 Reserve a few raspberries for decoration, then layer the remainder with the oat mixture in four stemmed glasses. Cover and chill for 2 hours.

5 About 30 minutes before serving, remove the glasses from the refrigerator to bring to room temperature. Decorate with the reserved raspberries and mint sprigs.

Cook's Tip

For finger biscuits to serve with the dessert, cream 150g/5oz/ 10 tbsp butter with 75g/3oz/6 tbsp caster (superfine) sugar until light and fluffy, then beat in an egg, a few drops of almond extract and 225g/8oz/2 cups plain (all-purpose) flour. Spoon into a piping (pastry) bag, fitted with a plain nozzle, and pipe 7.5cm/3in fingers on to baking sheets lined with baking parchment. Bake at 230°C/450°F/Gas 8 for 5 minutes. Cool.

Old English Trifle

This old-fashioned dessert never fails to please. If you are making it for children, replace the sherry and brandy with orange juice.

Serves 6

75g/3oz day-old sponge (pound) cake, broken into bitesize pieces
8 ratafia biscuits (almond macaroons), broken into halves
100ml/3½fl oz/⅓ cup medium sherry
30ml/2 tbsp brandy
350g/12oz/3 cups prepared fruit such as raspberries, peaches or strawberries

300ml/½ pint/1¼ cups double (heavy) cream
40g/1½oz/scant ½ cup toasted flaked (sliced) almonds, to decorate
strawberries, to decorate

For the custard

4 egg yolks
25g/1oz/2 tbsp caster (superfine) sugar
450ml/¾ pint/scant 2 cups single (light) or whipping cream
a few drops of vanilla extract

1 Put the sponge cake and ratafias in a glass serving dish, then sprinkle over the sherry and brandy and leave until they have been absorbed.

2 To make the custard, whisk the egg yolks and caster sugar together. Bring the cream to the boil in a heavy pan, then pour on to the egg yolk mixture, stirring constantly.

3 Return the mixture to the pan and heat very gently, stirring all the time with a wooden spoon, until the custard thickens enough to coat the back of the spoon; do not allow to boil. Stir in the vanilla extract. Leave to cool, stirring occasionally.

4 Put the fruit in an even layer over the sponge cake and ratafias in the serving dish, then strain the custard over the fruit and leave to set.

5 Lightly whip the cream, then spread it evenly over the custard. Chill the trifle well. Decorate with flaked almonds and strawberries just before serving.

Cranachan Energy 512kcal/2126kJ; Protein 4g; Carbohydrate 25.9g, of which sugars 16.8g; Fat 41.6g, of which saturates 25.1g; Cholesterol 103mg; Calcium 66mg; Fibre 3.1g; Sodium 25mg.
Trifle Energy 764kcal/3160kJ; Protein 7.7g; Carbohydrate 23.2g, of which sugars 17.4g; Fat 68.9g, of which saturates 38.1g; Cholesterol 296mg; Calcium 135mg; Fibre 2.2g; Sodium 106mg.

Peach Melba

The original dish created for the opera singer Dame Nellie Melba had peaches and ice cream served in grand style upon an ice swan.

Serves 4
300g/11oz/scant 2 cups fresh
    raspberries

squeeze of lemon juice
icing (confectioners') sugar,
    to taste
2 large ripe peaches or
    425g/15oz can sliced peaches
8 scoops vanilla ice cream

1 Press the raspberries through a non-metallic sieve (strainer) to form a purée.

2 Add a little lemon juice to the raspberry purée and sweeten to taste with icing sugar.

3 If using fresh peaches, cover them with boiling water for 4–5 seconds, then slip off the skins. Halve the peaches along the indented line, then slice neatly. If using canned peaches, place them in a strainer and drain them well.

4 Place two scoops of ice cream in each of 4 individual glass dishes, top with peach slices, then pour over the raspberry purée. Serve immediately.

Cook's Tip
For homemade vanilla ice cream, put 300ml/½ pint/1¼ cups milk in a heavy pan, with a split vanilla pod (bean). Bring to the boil, then remove from the heat and leave for 15 minutes. Remove the pod and scrape the seeds into the milk. Whisk 4 egg yolks with 75g/3oz/6 tbsp caster (superfine) sugar and 5ml/1 tsp cornflour (cornstarch) until thick and foamy. Gradually whisk in the hot milk. Return to the pan and cook, stirring, until thick. Cool. Whip 300ml/½ pint/1¼ cups double (heavy) cream until thick; fold into the custard. Pour into a freezer container. Freeze for 6 hours or until firm, beating twice during this time.

Summer Pudding

Unbelievably simple to make and totally delicious, this is a real warm weather classic. It's also a productive way of using up leftover bread.

Serves 4
about 8 thin slices white bread,
    at least one day old
800g/1¾lb mixed summer fruits
about 30ml/2 tbsp granulated
    sugar

1 Remove the crusts from the bread. Cut a round from one slice of bread to fit in the base of a 1.2 litre/2 pint/5 cup round, deep bowl and place in position. Cut strips of bread about 5cm/2in wide and use to line the sides of the bowl, overlapping the strips as you work.

2 Place the fruit, sugar and 30ml/2 tbsp water in a large heavy pan and heat gently, shaking the pan occasionally, until the fruit juices begin to run.

3 Reserve about 45ml/3 tbsp fruit juice and some fruit for decoration, then spoon the remaining fruit and juice into the prepared bowl, taking care not to dislodge the bread lining.

4 Cut the remaining bread to fit entirely over the fruit. Stand the bowl on a plate and cover with a saucer or small plate that will just fit inside the top of the bowl. Place a heavy weight on top. Chill the pudding and the reserved fruit juice overnight.

5 Run a knife carefully around the inside of the bowl rim, then invert the pudding on to a cold serving plate. Pour over the reserved juice, making sure that all the bread is completely covered, top with the reserved fruit and serve.

Cook's Tips
• *Use a good mix of summer fruits for this pudding – red and blackcurrants, raspberries, strawberries and loganberries.*
• *Summer pudding freezes well so make an extra one to enjoy during the winter.*

Peach Melba Energy 256kcal/1078kJ; Protein 6.1g; Carbohydrate 32.9g, of which sugars 31.6g; Fat 10.6g, of which saturates 7.4g; Cholesterol 29mg; Calcium 144mg; Fibre 3g; Sodium 75mg.
Pudding Energy 206kcal/872kJ; Protein 6.2g; Carbohydrate 45.2g, of which sugars 19.9g; Fat 1.2g, of which saturates 0g; Cholesterol 0mg; Calcium 95mg; Fibre 3g; Sodium 293mg.

Raspberries with Fruit Purée

Three colourful fruit purées, swirled together, make a kaleidoscopic garnish for a nest of raspberries.

Serves 4–6
200g/7oz/1¼ cups raspberries
120ml/4fl oz/½ cup red wine
icing (confectioners') sugar,
  for dusting

For the decoration
1 large mango, peeled and
  chopped
400g/14oz kiwi fruit, peeled and
  chopped
200g/7oz/1¼ cups raspberries
icing (confectioners') sugar,
  to taste
hazlenut cookies, to serve

1 Place the raspberries in a bowl with the red wine and allow to macerate for about 2 hours.

2 To make the decoration, purée the mango in a food processor, adding water if necessary. Press through a sieve (strainer) into a bowl. Purée the kiwi fruit in the same way, then make a third purée from the remaining raspberries. Sweeten the purées with sifted icing sugar, if necessary.

3 Spoon each purée on to a serving plate, separating the kiwi and mango with the raspberry purée as if creating a four-wedged pie. Gently tap the plate on the work surface to settle the purées against each other.

4 Using a skewer, draw a spiral outwards from the centre of the plate to the rim. Drain the macerated raspberries, pile them in the centre, and dust them heavily with icing sugar.

> **Cook's Tip**
> For hazelnut bites, cream 115g/4oz/½ cup butter with 75g/3oz/⅔ cup icing (confectioners') sugar until light and fluffy. Beat in 115g/4oz/1 cup flour, 75g/3oz/¾ cup ground hazelnuts and 1 egg yolk. Shape into small balls and place on lined baking sheets. Press a hazelnut into the centre of each. Bake at 180°C/350°F/Gas 4 for 10 minutes and allow to cool.

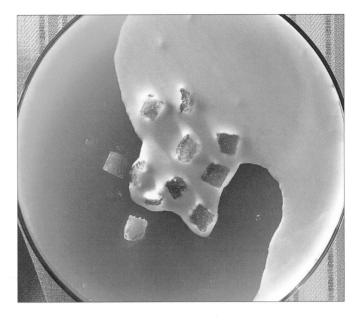

Apricot & Orange Jelly

This refreshing jelly is the perfect way to round off a summer. Decorate with slivers of fresh apricot or blanched orange rind shreds, if you prefer.

Serves 4
350g/12oz well-flavoured fresh
  ripe apricots, stoned (pitted)
50–75g/2–3oz/about ⅓ cup
  sugar
about 300ml/½ pint/1¼ cups
  freshly squeezed orange juice
15ml/1 tbsp powdered gelatine
single (light) cream, to serve
finely chopped candied orange
  peel, to decorate

1 Heat the apricots, sugar and 120ml/4fl oz/½ cup of the orange juice, stirring until the sugar has dissolved. Simmer gently until the apricots are tender.

2 Press the apricot mixture through a nylon sieve (strainer) into a small measuring jug (cup).

3 Pour 45ml/3 tbsp of the orange juice into a small heatproof bowl, sprinkle over the gelatine and leave for about 5 minutes, until spongy.

4 Place the bowl over a pan of hot water and heat until the gelatine has dissolved. Slowly pour into the apricot mixture, stirring, constantly. Make up to 600ml/1 pint/2½ cups with the remaining orange juice.

5 Pour the apricot mixture into four individual dishes and chill in the refrigerator until set.

6 Just before serving, pour a thin layer of cream over the surface of the jellies and decorate with candied orange peel.

> **Variation**
> You could also make this light dessert with nectarines or peaches instead of the apricots.

Fruit Purée Energy 69kcal/294kJ; Protein 1.7g; Carbohydrate 11.9g, of which sugars 11.7g; Fat 0.5g, of which saturates 0.1g; Cholesterol 0mg; Calcium 34mg; Fibre 3.3g; Sodium 6mg.
Orange Jelly Energy 116kcal/496kJ; Protein 4.4g; Carbohydrate 26g, of which sugars 26g; Fat 0.2g, of which saturates 0g; Cholesterol 0mg; Calcium 27mg; Fibre 1.6g; Sodium 10mg.

Raspberry Passion Fruit Swirls

If passion fruit is not available, this simple dessert can be made with raspberries alone.

Serves 4
300g/11oz/generous 2½ cups raspberries

2 passion fruit
350ml/12fl oz/1½ cups Greek (US strained plain) yogurt
25g/1oz/2 tbsp caster (superfine) sugar
raspberries and sprigs of fresh mint, to decorate

1 Mash the raspberries in a small bowl with a fork until the juice runs. Scoop out the passion fruit pulp into a separate bowl, add the yogurt and sugar and mix well.

2 Spoon alternate spoonfuls of the raspberry pulp and the yogurt mixture into stemmed glasses or one large serving dish, stirring lightly to create a swirled effect.

3 Decorate the desserts with whole raspberries and sprigs of fresh mint. Serve chilled.

Frudités with Honey Dip

A colourful and tasty variation on the popular savoury crudités, this dessert is great fun for impromptu entertaining. Use any combination of fresh fruit you wish.

Serves 4
225g/8oz/1 cup Greek (US strained plain) yogurt
45ml/3 tbsp clear honey
selection of fruits such as apples, grapes, strawberries, peaches and cherries, for dipping

1 Place the yogurt in a dish, beat until smooth, then stir in the honey, leaving a marbled effect.

2 Cut a selection of fruits into wedges or bitesize pieces or leave whole, depending on your choice. Arrange on a platter with the bowl of dip in the centre. Chill before serving.

Creamy Mango Cheesecake

This low-fat cheesecake is as creamy as any other, but makes a healthier dessert option – so there's no need to hold back!

Serves 4
115g/4oz/1¼ cups rolled oats
40g/1½ oz/3 tbsp sunflower margarine
30ml/2 tbsp clear honey

1 large ripe mango
300g/10oz/1¼ cups low-fat soft cheese
150ml/¼ pint/⅔ cup low-fat natural (plain) yogurt
finely grated rind of 1 small lime
45ml/3 tbsp apple juice
20ml/4 tsp powdered gelatine
fresh mango and lime slices, to decorate

1 Preheat the oven to 200°C/400°F/Gas 6. Place the rolled oats in a mixing bowl and add the margarine and honey. Mix well together, then press into the base of a 20cm/8in loose-bottomed cake tin (pan).

2 Bake the oat base for 12–15 minutes, then remove the tin from the oven and leave to cool.

3 Peel, stone (pit) and roughly chop the mango. Place in a food processor or blender with the cheese, yogurt and lime rind and process until smooth.

4 Put the apple juice in a small pan and place over heat until boiling. Remove from the heat, sprinkle the gelatine over the apple juice, then stir until dissolved. Stir into the mango and cheese mixture.

5 Pour into the tin and chill until set. Remove from the tin and decorate with mango and lime slices.

> **Cook's Tip**
> For a richer, no-cook base, process 150g/5oz/1½ cups digestive biscuits (graham crackers) to form crumbs. Melt 40g/1½oz/ 3 tbsp butter, stir in the crumbs, then press into the tin and chill.

Swirls Energy 97kcal/414kJ; Protein 8g; Carbohydrate 16.4g, of which sugars 16.4g; Fat 0.4g, of which saturates 0.2g; Cholesterol 1mg; Calcium 99mg; Fibre 2.1g; Sodium 33mg.
Frudités Energy 97kcal/407kJ; Protein 3.7g; Carbohydrate 9.7g, of which sugars 9.7g; Fat 5.7g, of which saturates 2.9g; Cholesterol 0mg; Calcium 85mg; Fibre 0g; Sodium 41mg.
Cheesecake Energy 373kcal/1567kJ; Protein 21.2g; Carbohydrate 38.6g, of which sugars 17.6g; Fat 17.1g, of which saturates 4.1g; Cholesterol 19mg; Calcium 180mg; Fibre 2.9g; Sodium 451mg.

Boston Banoffee Pie

This dessert's rich, creamy, toffee-style filling just can't be resisted – but who cares!

Serves 4–6
For the pastry
150g/5oz/1¼ cups plain (all-purpose) flour
115g/4oz/½ cup butter, diced
50g/2oz/¼ cup caster (superfine) sugar

For the filling
115g/4oz/½ cup butter, diced
½ x 400g/14oz can skimmed, sweetened condensed milk
115g/4oz/⅔ cup soft light brown sugar
30ml/2 tbsp golden (light corn) syrup
2 small bananas, sliced
a little lemon juice
whipped cream and grated chocolate, to decorate

I Preheat the oven to 160°C/325°F/Gas 3. To make the pastry, put the flour in a bowl and rub in the butter until the mixture resembles coarse breadcrumbs. Stir in the caster sugar and squeeze together to form a dough.

2 Press into the base of a 20cm/8in loose-based fluted flan tin (pan). Chill for 15 minutes.

3 Line the chilled pastry case (pie shell) with baking parchment and baking beans, then bake blind for 15 minutes. Remove the paper and beans and bake for a further 15 minutes, until crisp and golden. Leave to cool in the tin.

4 To make the filling, put the butter, condensed milk, brown sugar and syrup into a non-stick pan and heat gently, stirring, until the butter has melted and the sugar has dissolved.

5 Bring to a gentle boil and cook for 7 minutes, stirring constantly, until the mixture thickens and turns a light caramel colour. Pour into the cooled pastry case and leave until cold.

6 Sprinkle the bananas with lemon juice and arrange in overlapping circles on top of the caramel filling, leaving a gap in the centre. Pipe a swirl of whipped cream in the centre and sprinkle with grated chocolate.

Strawberry & Blueberry Tart

This tart works equally well using either autumn or winter fruits as long as there is a riot of colour.

Serves 6–8
For the pastry
225g/8oz/2 cups plain (all-purpose) flour
pinch of salt
75g/3oz/⅔ cup icing (confectioners') sugar
150g/5oz/generous ½ cup unsalted (sweet) butter
1 egg yolk

For the filling
350g/12oz/1¾ cups mascarpone
30ml/2 tbsp icing (confectioners') sugar
few drops of vanilla extract
finely grated rind of 1 orange
450–675g/1–1½ lb/4½ cups fresh mixed strawberries and blueberries
90ml/6 tbsp redcurrant jelly
30ml/2 tbsp orange juice

I Sift the flour, salt and sugar into a bowl. Dice the butter and rub it in until the mixture resembles coarse breadcrumbs. Mix in the egg yolk and 10ml/2 tsp cold water. Gather the dough together, knead lightly, wrap and chill for 1 hour.

2 Preheat the oven to 190°C/375°F/Gas 5. Roll out the pastry and use to line a 25cm/10in fluted flan tin (pan). Prick the base and chill for 15 minutes.

3 Line the chilled pastry case (pie shell) with baking parchment and baking beans, then bake blind for 15 minutes. Remove the paper and beans and bake for a further 15 minutes, until crisp and golden. Leave to cool in the tin.

4 To make the filling, beat together the mascarpone, sugar, vanilla extract and orange rind in a mixing bowl until smooth.

5 Remove the pastry case from the tin, then spoon in the filling and pile the fruits on top.

6 Heat the redcurrant jelly with the orange juice until runny, sieve, then brush over the fruit to form a glaze.

Pie Energy 582kcal/2437kJ; Protein 5.8g; Carbohydrate 74g, of which sugars 58.8g; Fat 31.2g, of which saturates 19.6g; Cholesterol 80mg; Calcium 161mg; Fibre 0.9g; Sodium 293mg.
Tart Energy 419kcal/1753kJ; Protein 7.8g; Carbohydrate 48.5g, of which sugars 27.1g; Fat 22.9g, of which saturates 14g; Cholesterol 84mg; Calcium 63mg; Fibre 1.5g; Sodium 123mg.

DESSERTS

Floating Islands in Plum Sauce

This unusual dessert is simpler to make than it looks, and is quite delicious. It also has the added bonus of being low in fat.

Serves 4
450g/1lb red plums
300ml/½ pint/1¼ cups apple juice
2 egg whites
30ml/2 tbsp concentrated apple juice syrup
pinch of freshly grated nutmeg (optional)

1 Halve the plums and remove the stones (pits). Place them in a wide pan with the apple juice.

2 Bring to the boil, then cover with a tight-fitting lid and leave to simmer gently until the plums are tender.

3 Meanwhile, place the egg whites in a grease-free, dry bowl and whisk until stiff peaks form.

4 Gradually whisk in the apple juice syrup, whisking until the meringue holds fairly firm peaks.

5 To make the "islands", use a tablespoon to scoop the meringue mixture carefully into the gently simmering plum sauce. (You may need to cook them in two batches.)

6 Cover again and allow to simmer gently for 2–3 minutes, until the meringues are just set. Serve immediately, sprinkled with a little freshly grated nutmeg.

Cook's Tip
• *A bottle of concentrated apple juice is a useful store-cupboard sweetener, but if you don't have any, just use a little honey instead.*
• *This is useful for entertaining as the plum sauce can be made in advance and reheated just before you cook the meringues.*

Souffléed Rice Pudding

The fluffy egg whites in this unusually light rice pudding make the portions seem much more substantial, without adding lots of extra unwanted fat.

Serves 4
65g/2½ oz/⅓ cup short grain pudding rice
45ml/3 tbsp clear honey
750ml/1¼ pints/3 cups semi-skimmed milk
1 vanilla pod (bean) or 2.5ml/ ½ tsp vanilla extract
2 egg whites
5ml/1 tsp finely grated nutmeg

1 Place the pudding rice, clear honey and the milk in a heavy or non-stick pan and bring to the boil. Add the vanilla pod, if using.

2 Lower the heat and cover with a tight-fitting lid. Leave to simmer gently for about 1–1¼ hours, stirring occasionally to prevent sticking, until most of the liquid has been absorbed.

3 Remove the vanilla pod from the pan, or if using vanilla extract, add this to the rice mixture now. Set aside so that the mixture cools slightly. Preheat the oven to 220°C/425°F/Gas 7.

4 Place the egg whites in a clean dry bowl and whisk until stiff peaks form.

5 Using a metal spoon or spatula, fold the egg whites evenly into the rice mixture and turn into a 1 litre/1¾ pint/4 cup ovenproof dish.

6 Sprinkle with grated nutmeg and bake for 15–20 minutes, until the pudding is well risen and golden brown.

Cook's Tip
You can use skimmed milk instead of semi-skimmed if you like, but take care when it is simmering as, with so little fat, it tends to boil over very easily.

Islands Energy 94kcal/406kJ; Protein 2.2g; Carbohydrate 22.5g, of which sugars 22.5g; Fat 0.2g, of which saturates 0g; Cholesterol 0mg; Calcium 22mg; Fibre 1.8g; Sodium 38mg.
Pudding Energy 183kcal/773kJ; Protein 9.1g; Carbohydrate 30.4g, of which sugars 17.4g; Fat 3.3g, of which saturates 2g; Cholesterol 11mg; Calcium 230mg; Fibre 0g; Sodium 112mg.

Cabinet Pudding

Rich custard is baked with dried fruit and sponge cake to make a delightful old-fashioned dessert that is sure to cause a stir.

Serves 4
25g/1oz/2½ tbsp raisins, chopped
30ml/2 tbsp brandy (optional)
25g/1oz glacé (candied) cherries, halved
25g/1oz angelica, chopped
2 trifle sponge (pound) cakes
50g/2oz ratafias (almond macaroons)
2 eggs
2 egg yolks
25g/1oz/2 tbsp sugar
450ml/¾ pint/1¾ cups single (light) cream or milk
few drops of vanilla extract

1 Soak the raisins in the brandy, if using, for several hours.

2 Butter a 750ml/1¼ pint/3 cup charlotte mould and arrange some of the cherries and angelica in the base.

3 Dice the sponge cakes and crush the ratafias. Mix with the remaining cherries and angelica, raisins and brandy, if using, and spoon into the mould.

4 Lightly whisk together the eggs, egg yolks and sugar. Bring the cream or milk just to the boil, then stir into the egg mixture with the vanilla extract.

5 Strain the egg mixture into the mould, then set aside for 15–30 minutes. Preheat the oven to 160°C/325°F/Gas 3.

6 Place the mould in a roasting pan. Cover with baking parchment and pour boiling water into the roasting pan. Bake for 1 hour, or until set. Leave for 2–3 minutes, then loosen the edge with a knife and turn out on to a warmed plate.

> **Cook's Tip**
> If you do not have a traditional charlotte mould, you can use a deep round cake tin (pan) instead.

Eve's Pudding

The apples beneath the topping are the reason for this pudding's name.

Serves 4–6
115g/4oz/½ cup butter, softened
115g/4oz/generous ½ cup caster (superfine) sugar
2 eggs, beaten
grated rind and juice of 1 lemon
90g/3½ oz/scant 1 cup self-raising (self-rising) flour
40g/1½ oz/generous ¼ cup ground almonds
115g/4oz/½ cup soft brown sugar
500–675g/1½ lb cooking apples, cored and thinly sliced
25g/1oz/¼ cup flaked (sliced) almonds
ready-made fresh custard or single (light) cream, to serve

1 Beat together the butter and caster sugar in a large mixing bowl until the mixture is very light and fluffy.

2 Gradually beat the eggs into the butter mixture, beating well after each addition, then fold in the lemon rind, flour and ground almonds.

3 Mix the brown sugar with the apples and lemon juice in a bowl, then turn into an ovenproof dish. Spoon the topping mixture on top of the apples, levelling the surface, then sprinkle with the flaked almonds.

4 Bake for 40–45 minutes, until golden. Serve immediately with fresh custard or cream.

> **Variations**
> • To ring the changes, replace half the apples with fresh blackberries. Halved apricots and sliced peaches can also be used instead of the apples.
> • To vary the topping, leave out the ground and flaked almonds and use demerara (raw) sugar instead of the caster sugar, then serve sprinkled with icing (confectioners') sugar.

Cabinet Energy 424kcal/1769kJ; Protein 10.5g; Carbohydrate 31.3g, of which sugars 23.1g; Fat 29.5g, of which saturates 16.2g; Cholesterol 286mg; Calcium 160mg; Fibre 0.5g; Sodium 128mg.
Eve's Energy 697kcal/2926kJ; Protein 9.5g; Carbohydrate 90g, of which sugars 72.4g; Fat 35.9g, of which saturates 16.5g; Cholesterol 156mg; Calcium 126mg; Fibre 3.9g; Sodium 218mg.

Apple & Orange Pie

A tasty variation of an old favourite, this easy-to-make two-fruit pie will be a big hit. Make sure you choose really juicy oranges or even blood oranges for succulent results. It's delicious served with lashings of cream.

Serves 4
400g/14oz ready-made shortcrust (unsweetened) pastry
3 oranges, peeled
900g/2lb cooking apples, cored and thickly sliced
25g/1oz/2 tbsp demerara (raw) sugar
beaten egg, to glaze
caster (superfine) sugar, for sprinkling

1 Roll out the pastry on a lightly floured surface to about 2cm/¾in larger than the top of a 1.2 litre/2 pint/5 cup pie dish. Cut off a narrow strip around the edge of the pastry and fit on the rim of the pie dish.

2 Preheat the oven to 190°C/375°F/Gas 5. Hold one orange at a time over a bowl to catch the juice, and cut down between the membranes to remove the segments.

3 Mix the orange segments and juice, the apples and sugar in the pie dish. Place a pie funnel in the centre of the dish.

4 Dampen the pastry strip. Cover the dish with the rolled out pastry and press the edges to the pastry strip. Brush the top with beaten egg, then bake for 35–40 minutes, until lightly browned. Sprinkle with caster sugar before serving.

> **Cook's Tip**
> If you have time, make your own shortcrust pastry. Sift 225g/8oz/2 cups plain (all-purpose) flour and a pinch of salt into a bowl. Add 115g/4oz/½ cup diced butter and rub in with your fingertips until the mixture resembles breadcrumbs. Mix to a dough with about 45ml/3 tbsp cold water, then wrap and chill for 30 minutes before rolling out as above.

Lemon Meringue Pie

In this popular dish, a light meringue topping crowns a delicious citrus-filled pie.

Serves 4
50g/2oz/¼ cup butter, diced
115g/4oz/1 cup plain (all-purpose) flour
25g/1oz/3 tbsp ground almonds
25g/1oz/2 tbsp caster (superfine) sugar
1 egg yolk

For the filling
juice of 3 lemons
finely grated rind of 2 lemons
45ml/3 tbsp cornflour (cornstarch)
75g/3oz/generous ¼ cup caster (superfine) sugar
2 egg yolks
15g/½oz/1 tbsp butter

For the meringue
2 egg whites
115g/4oz/½ cup caster (superfine) sugar

1 Rub the butter into the flour until the mixture resembles breadcrumbs. Stir in the almonds and sugar, then add the egg yolk and 30ml/2 tbsp cold water. Mix until the pastry comes together. Knead on a lightly floured surface, then wrap in cling film (plastic wrap) and chill for about 30 minutes.

2 Preheat a baking sheet at 200°C/400°F/Gas 6. Roll out the pastry and use to line a 18.5cm/7½in fluted loose-based flan tin (pan). Prick the base. Line with baking parchment and fill with baking beans. Place the tin on the baking sheet and bake blind for 12 minutes. Remove the paper and beans and bake for a further 5 minutes. Allow to cool. Reduce the temperature to 150°C/300°F/Gas 2.

3 To make the filling, blend the lemon juice, rind and cornflour. Pour into a pan and add 150ml/¼ pint/⅔ cup water. Bring to the boil, stirring until smooth and thickened. Remove and beat in the sugar and egg yolks, then add the butter. Spoon into the pastry case (pie shell).

4 To make the meringue, whisk the egg whites until stiff, then gradually whisk in the sugar until thick and glossy. Pile on top of the filling. Bake for 30–35 minutes, or until golden.

Meringue Energy 2180kcal/9185kJ; Protein 29.4g; Carbohydrate 357.5g, of which sugars 227.8g; Fat 80.2g, of which saturates 38.4g; Cholesterol 542mg; Calcium 403mg; Fibre 5.5g; Sodium 577mg.
Orange Pie Energy 610kcal/2566kJ; Protein 8.1g; Carbohydrate 86.1g, of which sugars 40.2g; Fat 28.5g, of which saturates 8.8g; Cholesterol 14mg; Calcium 168mg; Fibre 8.1g; Sodium 413mg.

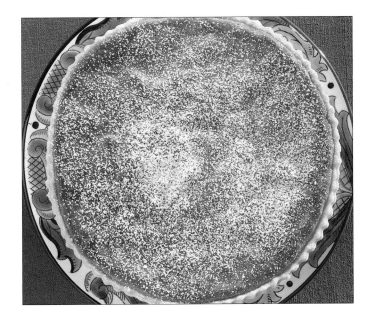

Bakewell Tart

This classic tart, with its crisp pastry base and delicious almond sponge filling, is always popular.

Serves 4
225g/8oz ready-made puff pastry
30ml/2 tbsp raspberry or
    apricot jam
2 eggs
2 egg yolks
115g/4oz/½ cup caster
    (superfine) sugar
115g/4oz/½ cup butter, melted
50g/2oz/⅔ cup ground almonds
few drops of almond extract
sifted icing (confectioners') sugar,
    for dredging

1 Preheat the oven to 200°C/400°F/Gas 6. Roll out the pastry on a lightly floured surface and use it to line an 18cm/7in pie plate or fluted loose-based flan tin (pan). Spread the jam over the base of the pastry case (pie shell).

2 Whisk the eggs, egg yolks and sugar together in a large bowl until thick and pale.

3 Gently stir the butter, ground almonds and almond extract into the egg mixture.

4 Pour the mixture into the pastry case and bake for about 30 minutes until the filling is just set and browned. Dredge with icing sugar before eating hot, warm or cold.

Cook's Tips
• Since the pastry case isn't baked blind first, place a baking sheet in the oven while it preheats, then place the pie dish or flan tin on the hot sheet. This will ensure that the base of the pastry case cooks through.
• Fresh, ready-made puff pastry is sold in the chilled section of supermarkets. Rich and buttery, puff pastry takes time and patience to make, as the method involves a drawn-out folding and rolling process. The ready-made version is more practical.
• Although the pastry base technically makes this a tart, the original recipe refers to it as a pudding.

Yorkshire Curd Tart

The distinguishing characteristic of this old-fashioned tart is the allspice, or "clove pepper" as it was once known locally. The tart is quite delicious, without tasting too sweet.

Serves 8
225g/8oz/2 cups plain
    (all-purpose) flour
115g/4oz/½ cup butter, diced
1 egg yolk
15–30ml/1–2 tbsp chilled water

For the filling
large pinch of allspice
90g/3½ oz/scant ½ cup soft
    light brown sugar
3 eggs, beaten
grated rind and juice of 1 lemon
40g/1½ oz/3 tbsp butter, melted
450g/1lb/2 cups curd cheese
75g/3oz/½ cup raisins or
    sultanas (golden raisins)
single (thin) cream, to serve
    (optional)

1 To make the pastry, place the flour in a mixing bowl. Add the butter and rub it into the flour with your fingertips until the mixture resembles breadcrumbs. Stir the egg yolk into the flour mixture with just enough of the water to bind to a dough.

2 Turn the dough on to a lightly floured surface, knead lightly and briefly, then form into a ball. Roll out the pastry thinly and use to line a 20cm/8in fluted loose-based flan tin (pan). Chill for 15 minutes in the refrigerator.

3 Meanwhile, preheat the oven to 190°C/375°F/Gas 5. To make the filling, mix the allspice with the sugar, then stir in the eggs, lemon rind and juice, melted butter, curd cheese and raisins.

4 Pour the filling into the pastry case (pie shell), then bake for about 40 minutes until the pastry is cooked and the filling is lightly set and golden. Serve warm, with cream, if you wish.

Cook's Tip
Although it is not traditional, mixed (apple pie) spice would make a good substitute for the ground allspice.

Bakewell Energy 701kcal/2922kJ; Protein 10.8g; Carbohydrate 57.1g, of which sugars 36.7g; Fat 50g, of which saturates 17.1g; Cholesterol 260mg; Calcium 110mg; Fibre 0.9g; Sodium 395mg.
Curd Tart Energy 480kcal/2005kJ; Protein 16.2g; Carbohydrate 48.2g, of which sugars 23.7g; Fat 27g, of which saturates 15.8g; Cholesterol 173mg; Calcium 153mg; Fibre 1.2g; Sodium 451mg.

Strawberry & Apple Crumble

A high-fibre, low-fat version of the classic apple crumble that will appeal to both children and adults alike.

2.5ml/½ tsp ground cinnamon
30ml/2 tbsp orange juice
natural (plain) yogurt, to
   serve (optional)

Serves 4
450g/1lb cooking apples
150g/5oz/1¼ cups strawberries,
   hulled
30ml/2 tbsp caster
   (superfine) sugar

For the crumble
45ml/3 tbsp plain wholemeal
   (whole-wheat) flour
50g/2oz/⅔ cup rolled oats
30ml/2 tbsp low-fat spread

1 Preheat the oven to 180°C/350°F/Gas 4. Peel, core and cut the apples into approximately 5mm/¼in size slices. Halve the strawberries.

2 Toss together the apples, strawberries, sugar, cinnamon and orange juice. Transfer the mixture to a 1.2 litre/2 pint/5 cup ovenproof dish.

3 To make the crumble, combine the flour and oats in a bowl and mix in the low-fat spread with a fork.

4 Sprinkle the crumble evenly over the fruit. Bake for 40–45 minutes, until golden brown and bubbling. Serve warm, with yogurt, if you like.

> **Cook's Tip**
> Use cooking apples rather than eating ones, as their soft cooked texture combines well with the crunchy topping.

> **Variation**
> Blackberries, raspberries or redcurrants can be used instead of the strawberries very successfully.

Castle Puddings with Custard Sauce

These attractive sponge puddings make a lovely finale to a dinner party.

2 eggs, beaten
few drops of vanilla extract
130g/4½ oz/generous 1 cup self-
   raising (self-rising) flour
mint sprigs, to decorate

Serves 4
about 45ml/3 tbsp blackcurrant,
   strawberry or raspberry jam
115g/4oz/½ cup butter, softened,
   plus extra for greasing
115g/4oz/generous ½ cup caster
   (superfine) sugar

For the custard sauce
4 eggs
15–25g/½ –1oz/1–2 tbsp sugar
450ml/¾ pint/scant 2 cups milk
few drops of vanilla extract

1 Preheat the oven to 180°C/350°F/Gas 4. Butter eight dariole moulds. Put about 10ml/2 tsp of your chosen jam in the base of each mould.

2 Beat the butter and sugar together until light and fluffy, then gradually beat in the eggs, beating well after each addition, and add the vanilla extract towards the end. Lightly fold in the flour, then divide the mixture among the moulds. Bake the puddings for about 20 minutes until well risen and a light golden colour.

3 To make the custard, whisk the eggs and sugar together. Bring the milk to the boil in a heavy, preferably non-stick, pan, then slowly pour on to the egg mixture, stirring constantly.

4 Return the milk mixture to the pan and heat very gently, stirring, until it thickens enough to coat the back of a spoon; do not allow to boil. Cover the pan and remove from the heat.

5 Remove the moulds from the oven. Leave to stand for a few minutes, then turn the puddings out on to warmed individual plates. Decorate with mint and serve with the custard.

> **Cook's Tip**
> If you do not have dariole moulds, use ramekin dishes instead.

Crumble Energy 200kcal/846kJ; Protein 3.8g; Carbohydrate 38.7g, of which sugars 21g; Fat 4.4g, of which saturates 0.9g; Cholesterol 0mg; Calcium 41mg; Fibre 3.4g; Sodium 59mg.
Puddings Energy 644kcal/2701kJ; Protein 16.7g; Carbohydrate 72.5g, of which sugars 47.7g; Fat 34.3g, of which saturates 18.6g; Cholesterol 353mg; Calcium 247mg; Fibre 1g; Sodium 334mg.

Easy Chocolate & Orange Soufflé

The base of this delicious soufflé is a simple semolina mixture, rather than the thick white sauce of most sweet soufflés. The finished dish looks most impressive.

Serve 4

butter, for greasing
600ml/1 pint/2½ cups milk
50g/2oz/scant ½ cup semolina
50g/2oz/¼ cup soft light brown sugar
grated rind of 1 orange
90ml/6 tbsp fresh orange juice
3 eggs, separated
65g/2½oz plain (semisweet) chocolate, grated
icing (confectioners') sugar, for sprinkling
pouring (half-and-half) cream, to serve (optional)

1 Preheat the oven to 200°C/400°F/Gas 6. Butter a shallow 1.75 litre/3 pint/7½ cup ovenproof dish.

2 Pour the milk into a heavy pan, sprinkle over the semolina and brown sugar, then heat, stirring the mixture constantly, until boiling and thickened.

3 Remove the pan from the heat; beat in the orange rind and juice, egg yolks and all but 15ml/1 tbsp of the chocolate.

4 Whisk the egg whites until stiff but not dry, then lightly fold one-third into the semolina mixture. Fold in the remaining egg white in two batches.

5 Spoon the mixture into the dish and bake for about 30 minutes until just set in the centre and risen.

6 Sprinkle the top with the remaining chocolate and icing sugar, then serve immediately with pouring cream, if you wish.

> **Variation**
> For a sophisticated touch, replace 15ml/1 tbsp of the orange juice with the same amount of orange-flavoured liqueur, such as Cointreau or Grand Marnier.

Chocolate Amaretti Peaches

This dessert is quick and easy to prepare, yet sophisticated enough to serve at the most elegant dinner party.

Serves 4

115g/4oz amaretti, crushed
50g/2oz plain (semisweet) chocolate, chopped
grated rind of ½ orange
15ml/1 tbsp clear honey
1.5ml/¼ tsp ground cinnamon
1 egg white, lightly beaten
4 firm ripe peaches
butter, for greasing
150ml/¼ pint/⅔ cup white wine
15g/½ oz/1 tbsp caster (superfine) sugar
whipped cream, to serve

1 Preheat the oven to 190°C/375°F/Gas 5. Mix together the crushed amaretti, chocolate, orange rind, honey and cinnamon in a bowl. Add the beaten egg white and mix to bind the mixture together.

2 Halve and stone (pit) the peaches and fill the cavities with the chocolate mixture, mounding it up slightly.

3 Arrange the stuffed peaches in a lightly buttered shallow ovenproof dish which will just hold the fruit comfortably. Pour the wine into a measuring jug and stir in the sugar.

4 Pour the wine mixture around the peaches. Bake for 30–40 minutes, until the peaches are tender. Serve with a little of the cooking juices spooned over and the whipped cream.

> **Cook's Tip**
> Italian amaretti are crisp little cookies, flavoured with bitter almonds. They are now available from supermarkets.

> **Variation**
> This dessert can also be prepared using fresh nectarines or apricots instead of peaches. Use 2 apricots per person.

Soufflé Energy 308kcal/1300kJ; Protein 12.1g; Carbohydrate 42.1g, of which sugars 32.3g; Fat 11.5g, of which saturates 5.5g; Cholesterol 153mg; Calcium 218mg; Fibre 0.7g; Sodium 123mg.
Peaches Energy 275kcal/1163kJ; Protein 4g; Carbohydrate 45.3g, of which sugars 32.7g; Fat 7.4g, of which saturates 3.8g; Cholesterol 1mg; Calcium 55mg; Fibre 2.2g; Sodium 114mg.

Bread & Butter Pudding

An unusual version of a classic recipe, this pudding is made with French bread and mixed dried fruit. As a finishing touch, it is served with a whisky-flavoured cream.

Serves 4–6

4 ready-to-eat dried apricots, finely chopped
15ml/1 tbsp raisins
30ml/2 tbsp sultanas (golden raisins)
15ml/1 tbsp chopped mixed (candied) peel
1 French loaf (about 200g/7oz), thinly sliced
50g/2oz/¼ cup butter, melted, plus extra for greasing

450ml/¾ pint/scant 2 cups milk
150ml/¼ pint/⅔ cup double (heavy) cream
115g/4oz/½ cup caster (superfine) sugar
3 eggs
2.5ml/½ tsp vanilla extract
30ml/2 tbsp whisky

For the cream

150ml/¼ pint/⅔ cup double (heavy) cream
30ml/2 tbsp Greek-style (US strained, plain) yogurt
15–30ml/1–2 tbsp whisky
15g/½oz/1 tbsp caster (superfine) sugar

1 Preheat the oven to 180°C/350°F/Gas 4. Butter a deep 1.5 litre/2½ pint/6¼ cup ovenproof dish. Mix together the dried fruits. Brush the bread on both sides with butter.

2 Fill the dish with alternate layers of bread and dried fruit, starting with fruit and finishing with bread. Heat the milk and cream in a pan until just boiling. Whisk together the sugar, eggs and vanilla extract.

3 Whisk the milk mixture into the eggs, then strain into the dish. Sprinkle the whisky over the top. Press the bread down, cover with foil and leave to stand for 20 minutes.

4 Place the foil-covered dish in a roasting pan, half filled with water, and bake for 1 hour, or until the custard is just set. Remove the foil and cook for 10 minutes more until golden.

5 Just before serving, heat all the cream ingredients in a small pan, stirring. Serve with the hot pudding.

Sticky Toffee Pudding

Filling, warming and packed with calories, this delightfully gooey steamed pudding is still a firm favourite.

Serves 6

115g/4oz/1 cup toasted walnuts, chopped
175g/6oz/¾ cup butter, plus extra for greasing

175g/6oz/1 cup soft brown sugar
60ml/4 tbsp double (heavy) cream
30ml/2 tbsp lemon juice
2 eggs, beaten
115g/4oz/1 cup self-raising (self-rising) flour

1 Grease a 900ml/1½ pint/3¾ cup heatproof deep bowl and add half the chopped nuts.

2 Heat 50g/2oz/¼ cup of the butter with 50g/2oz/¼ cup of the sugar, the cream and 15ml/1 tbsp of the lemon juice in a small pan, stirring until smooth. Pour half into the greased bowl, then swirl to coat it a little way up the sides. Reserve the rest of the sauce for serving.

3 Beat the remaining butter and sugar until light and fluffy, then gradually beat in the eggs. Fold in the flour and the remaining nuts and lemon juice and spoon into the bowl.

4 Cover the bowl with greaseproof (waxed) paper with a pleat folded in the centre, then tie securely with string.

5 Place the bowl in a pan with enough water to come halfway up the sides of the bowl. Cover with a lid and bring to the boil. Keep the water boiling gently and steam the pudding for 1¼ hours, topping up the water as required, until the pudding is completely set in the centre. Alternatively, steam the pudding in a steamer.

6 Just before serving, gently warm the reserved sauce. To serve, run a knife around the edge of the pudding to loosen it, then turn out on to a warm plate. Pour the warm sauce over the pudding and serve immediately.

Sticky toffee Energy 603kcal/2510kJ; Protein 7.2g; Carbohydrate 46.4g, of which sugars 31.6g; Fat 44.6g, of which saturates 20.2g; Cholesterol 139mg; Calcium 80mg; Fibre 1.3g; Sodium 206mg.
Bread & butter Energy 622kcal/2597kJ; Protein 10.5g; Carbohydrate 55.6g, of which sugars 37.8g; Fat 39g, of which saturates 23g; Cholesterol 186mg; Calcium 203mg; Fibre 1.6g; Sodium 350mg.

Plum & Walnut Crumble

Walnuts add a lovely crunch to the fruit layer in this rich and warming crumble. Serve with dollops of whipped cream for a tasty dessert.

Serves 4–6

75g/3oz/¾ cup walnut pieces
900g/2lb plums
175g/6oz/1 cup demerara (raw) sugar
75g/3oz/6 tbsp butter or hard margarine, cut into dice
175g/6oz/1½ cups plain (all-purpose) flour

1 Preheat the oven to 180°C/350°F/Gas 4. Spread the nuts on a baking sheet and place in the oven for 8–10 minutes until evenly coloured.

2 Butter a 1.2 litre/2 pint/5 cup baking dish. Halve and stone (pit) the plums, then put them into the dish and stir in the nuts and half of the demerara sugar.

3 Rub the butter or margarine into the flour until the mixture resembles coarse crumbs. Stir in the remaining sugar and continue to rub in until fine crumbs are formed.

4 Cover the fruit with the crumb mixture and press it down lightly. Bake the pudding for about 45 minutes, until the top is golden brown and the fruit tender.

Cook's Tip
For speed, use a food processor to rub the butter into the flour.

Variations
• *To make an oat and cinnamon crumble, substitute rolled oats for half the flour in the crumble mixture and add 2.5–5ml/ ½ –1 tsp ground cinnamon, to taste.*
• *Try replacing the walnuts with hazelnuts or almonds.*

Baked Rice Pudding

Ready-made rice pudding simply cannot compare with this creamy home-made version, especially if you like the golden skin.

Serves 4

50g/2oz/¼ cup short grain pudding rice
25g/1oz/2 tbsp soft light brown sugar
50g/2oz/¼ cup butter, plus extra for greasing
900ml/1½ pints/3¾ cups milk
small strip of lemon rind
pinch of freshly grated nutmeg
fresh mint sprigs, to decorate
raspberries, to serve (optional)

1 Preheat the oven to 150°C/300°F/Gas 2, then butter a 1.2 litre/2 pint/5 cup shallow baking dish.

2 Put the rice, sugar and butter into the prepared dish, then stir in the milk and lemon rind. Sprinkle a little nutmeg over the surface of the mixture.

3 Bake the rice pudding in the oven for about 2½ hours, stirring after 30 minutes and another couple of times during the next 2 hours until the rice is tender and the pudding has a thick and creamy consistency.

4 If you like skin on top, leave the rice pudding undisturbed for the final 30 minutes of cooking (otherwise, stir it again). Serve the rice pudding immediately, decorated with fresh mint sprigs and raspberries, if using.

Variations
• *Use 1.5ml/¼ tsp ground cinnamon or mixed spice instead of the grated nutmeg for a change of flavour.*
• *Baked rice pudding is even more delicious with fruit. Add some sultanas (golden raisins), raisins or chopped ready-to-eat dried apricots to the pudding, or serve it alongside sliced fresh peaches or nectarines, or whole fresh strawberries.*

Crumble Energy 325kcal/1361kJ; Protein 4.1g; Carbohydrate 36.5g, of which sugars 26.9g; Fat 19.2g, of which saturates 7.2g; Cholesterol 27mg; Calcium 58mg; Fibre 3.2g; Sodium 81mg.
Pudding Energy 266kcal/1114kJ; Protein 8.7g; Carbohydrate 27.2g, of which sugars 17.2g; Fat 14.2g, of which saturates 8.9g; Cholesterol 40mg; Calcium 278mg; Fibre 0g; Sodium 173mg.